Min

THE NEW
LITERATURE

Claude Mauriac

THE NEW LITERATURE

Translated by Samuel I. Stone

GEORGE BRAZILLER, INC., NEW YORK

1959

TO ANDRÉ SABATIER

Contents

INTRODUCTION 11
FRANZ KAFKA 15
ANTONIN ARTAUD 35
HENRY MILLER 51
MICHEL LEIRIS 61
SAMUEL BECKETT 75
GEORGES BATAILLE 91
ALBERT CAMUS 103
HENRI MICHAUX 119
GEORGES SIMENON 133
WLADIMIR WEIDLÉ 151
JEAN ROSTAND 161
ROGER CAILLOIS 175
ROLAND BARTHES 185
DIONYS MASCOLO 195
E. M. CIORAN 213
A. ROBBE-GRILLET 225
NATHALIE SARRAUTE 235
CONCLUSION 249

THE NEW LITERATURE

INTRODUCTION

THE EXPRESSIONS: "THAT'S LITERATURE" OR "THE REST IS literature," show to what degree of complacency the art of writing has too often fallen. Using the techniques of their day, and more or less following fashion, the best authors have always sought to transmit the inexpressible by means of literature but, as far as possible, without literature.

For this reason, I have coined the word *aliterature*, on the model of *amorality*. In this context *literature*, unlike *moral*, has an unfavorable connotation, and the α privative, instead of indicating a deficiency, on the contrary, designates a quality.

Aliterature (that is, literature freed from the hackneyed conventions which have given the word a pejorative meaning) is a never-reached pole, but honest writers have been going in its direction ever since there have been men, and among them, men who write. The history of literature and that of aliterature are parallel.

I have limited my objective in the present essay to contemporary aliterature, studied among certain of its most significant representatives: essayists, poets and novelists. We remember that M. Teste "relegated not only letters, but almost all philosophy as well, into the Vague Things or the Impure Things, which he wholeheartedly rejected." The young Paul Valéry saw in the *Discourse on Method* "the modern novel as it might have been." And Henri Mondor reports these words pronounced by the mature Valéry:

When a powerful alloy of literature, thought, and science, for one ought to know everything, has been realized by a man of genius, the productions of Edgar Poe himself will no longer appear as anything but tricks and virtuosity. . . . Of this language, enemy of the arbitrary and the hazy, the eulogy of Newton by Fontenelle might be ranked as a model, as well as certain pages of the *Discourse on Method.*

Thus, scorner of the novel that he was, Paul Valéry anticipated the modern novel, such as we see it in the first sketchy attempts today. But in exacting purity itself, one is always somebody's man-of-letters. Julien Benda interpreted the title *Variété* as indicating Valéry's intention (a specialist in precise mental clockwork if there ever was one) not to think with sequence or seriousness.

Aliterature avoids degenerating into literature only to fall into the opposite excess. A cry for help from Kafka, but a cry that is clearly worded, even if we are not always sure of understanding its meaning, may become incoherent when expressed by others.

After the silence of Rimbaud, the blank page of Mallarmé, the inarticulate cry of Artaud, aliterature finally dissolves in alliteration with Joyce. The author of *Finnegans Wake* in fact creates out of whole cloth words full of so many diverse overtones that they are eclipsed by them. For Beckett, on the contrary, words all say the same thing. In the extreme, it is by writing anything at all that this author best expresses what he considers important. The result is the same.

Kafka, Artaud, Beckett . . . We can study contemporary aliterature in no better way than to let them speak for themselves.

FRANZ KAFKA

IF FRANZ KAFKA FASCINATES INTELLECTUALS SO MUCH TODAY it is because he is "the stranger" par excellence. He felt at home nowhere, even in his native city, Prague. A Jew whose mother tongue was German, he was rejected by all non-Jewish circles and he sought in vain to be integrated into the Jewish community. Furthermore, it was especially in relation to himself that he was aware of this feeling of exclusion: a stranger to himself, even more than to the various social groups which encircled him like an unassimilable body.

This very sick man, stricken in both mind and body, personifies the imbalance of our times. He was one of the first to experience the *mal de siècle* that is so widespread today. His work prefigures that of most of the writers who are representative of our epoch. Not all of them have read him or have been influenced by him, but he was one of the first to be infected by this dangerous microbe.

Kafka's metaphysical affliction had a physical basis. Ever since adolescence, even before he contracted tuberculosis, he seems to have suffered from a kind of organic anxiety. He was never quite right in his mind. In the last year of his life he was to reproach himself for the hypochondria of his youth. Even then he had not been able to avoid the lure of unhappiness.

Literature, his literature, *bound word for word to his life,* was always the most effective of remedies at his disposal. He notes in his *Diaries:* "At this moment I have a great need to root out my anxiety by describing it completely, and as it comes from the depths of my being to transfer it to the depths of the paper." A moment that extended over his entire conscious existence.

Franz Kafka used to reproach himself for liking his comfort: "The chambermaid who forgets to bring me hot water in the morning upsets my world." [*Diaries*, 1922] But the fact is his world was perpetually in unstable equilibrium. From adolescence onward Kafka took notice of his coenesthesia. His body was affected before he became uneasy in his mind (and no doubt this is usually the case). He was one of those falsely yet truly sick people, like Marcel Proust, whom in the end (a premature end) we are surprised to see die. "The suffering that I endure, I endure in every respect. I have the doctor examine me and immediately he has the advantage of me. I literally become hollow, and he, despised and unrefuted, pours his empty speeches into me." [1913] This withdrawal into himself, regardless of any external evidence to the contrary, did not help him to find peace.

Metamorphosis is not just an apparently objective story. Kafka can write to Milena, the young translator of his work, with whom he had a passionate and difficult liaison: "My body is afraid, and rather than wait for proofs of kindness, which, in this sense, would truly save the world, it crawls along the wall, climbing slowly." Fear obsesses him. For him, to speak of love is first to speak of this fear, to load this fear, in the ever disappointed hope to be free of it, not upon the heart and body of Milena but upon her mind, so that he should no longer be alone in this knowledge. Knowledge of what? On this point, not only the *Letters to Milena* but the entire works of Kafka, including the *Diaries*, fail to enlighten us. And for the simple reason that all Kafka knew of his anguish was that it existed. We need but open the *Letters to Milena* at random. We find hardly a page in which fear is not present: "Without you, I have no one, no one here but Fear: sprawled over it as it sprawls over me, we toss through the nights clinging together!" Or again: "The only thing I know (about my fear) is the hand it places on my throat, and it is really the most terrible thing that I have ever lived through or could ever live through." The secret of his life lies there, but even if we unveil the secret, we don't know what it signifies. Our ignorance is, to a certain extent, like Kafka's:

I am still trying to communicate something that is uncommunicable, to explain something that is in my bones and can only be lived through in my bones. It is perhaps nothing else, fundamentally, but the famous fear of which I speak so often, but extended to everything: fear of the big, fear of the little; a convulsive fear to say a word. Though perhaps, to tell the truth, this fear is not solely fear, but a passionate desire for something greater than all which engenders it.

He notes in his *Diaries* in 1911 that he has ceased to be ashamed of his body. But this is not quite so, as letters of a far later period testify. His first complexes manifested themselves in connection with his overlong body which, he tells us, seemed borrowed from an odds-and-ends storeroom. Thanks to photographs we know his face and silhouette (whose ridiculousness he accentuated at times by willfully dressing in a grotesque fashion). That face, which, on one euphoric day, he admitted was "pure, harmoniously modeled, almost beautiful in its contours." Almost? Very. Very handsome: with that beauty which touches our hearts today when we come across pictures from Israel. A beauty that comes from the soul and which, in youth, the Jewish people approximates more than any other. We find also in these letters of his twenties the *long and thin individual* (121 pounds without clothes) whom he could not refrain from mocking. "I wouldn't dare hold out my hand to you, little girl, this dirty hand, trembling, clawlike, unsteady and self-conscious, this icy and burning hand."

We should not be surprised that he is little concerned with current events (even the Great War itself) in spite of his efforts to be interested in them. With but one or two exceptions, he sees Prague without making us see it, and changes this uniquely beautiful city into a sort of anonymous Kafkaian town under a spell of witchcraft. Corresponding to the terrible insecurity of his inner world (the expression is his) is the uncertainty of outside things and the impossibility, cruelly experienced, of communicating with human beings, aggravated by his ethnic background.

Mr. Willy Haas, who introduced the German edition of the *Letters to Milena,* after admitting that he had to make numerous deletions in the *Letters to Milena* for reasons of propriety (it is too bad that none of these suppressions is indicated in the text), adds: "On the other hand, and in spite of many hesitations, I have retained most of the passages concerning Judaism. For Kafka, the Jew, to love a non-Jewess was without doubt a great problem, etc." It is amazing that the question of these deletions could even have arisen. Deprived of this dimension, the drama of Kafka becomes even less comprehensible. The most significant passages, and also the most beautiful, in the *Letters to Milena* are the ones in which the author expresses the great sorrow of the Jews:

We both know plenty of typical examples of Western Jews; of all of them, I am, as far as I know, the most typical; this means, with a little exaggeration, that I do not have a second of peace, that nothing is given to me, that I must acquire everything, not only the present and the future but the past as well, something of which every man receives a share free; that, too, I must acquire, and that is perhaps the hardest task. . . .

At the age of thirty-eight he states: "Double it since I am a Jew." In Czech the question: "Are you a Jew?" is like a punch in the chest. Speaking to himself, he says: "You are after all a Jew and you know what fear is." It is no longer a question of the fear with which he was haunted, but of another kind of dread, more or less connected with the fact of being a Jew, no matter where perhaps, but especially in Central Europe:

Every afternoon now I take a walk in the streets; there they wallow in anti-Semitic hatred. I have just heard the Jews called "a race of lepers." Isn't it natural to leave a place where one is hated so much! (No need of Zionism or racism for that!) The heroism that consists in remaining in spite of everything resembles that of cockroaches which nothing drives out of bathrooms.

Looking through the window and seeing mounted police and gendarmes with bayonets on their guns holding back a howling mob, "he felt the horrible shame of living always under protection." To Milena he writes: "It remains dangerous to be a Jew, even at your feet." Another time, he explains to her that she must know that there is a part of one's fatherland that a man cannot forswear. But he, who has no country, he can renounce nothing, having nothing, being nothing. An unnamable animal climbing along a wall, he said; a cockroach; or again: "In the atmosphere of our common existence, I am only a mouse in the corner of a very large house, a mouse that is permitted, at the very most, to run across the carpet once a year." He begs his friend to allow him to return *into his hole.* "I would burrow in a dirty ditch anywhere at all (dirty by reason of my presence alone, naturally). . . ." A bestiary of Kafkaian humiliation: masochism as always closely intermixed with sadism.

This *torture,* which, as we shall see, is one of the keys to modern literature, is evoked many times by Kafka in his *Diaries.* And in the *Letters to Milena:* "Yes, torture is of great importance to me, I am occupied with nothing but torturing or being tortured." Before falling asleep, he would feel in the upper part of his skull a little cold flickering flame. He takes pleasure (it is he who uses the word pleasure) in imagining a knife which will turn itself around in his heart. [*Diaries,* 1911] Two years later, he is more specific: "Ceaselessly the image of a large pork-butcher's knife, which, starting at my side, chops into me with mechanical regularity and cuts out very thin slices which fly off." He has locks all over his body. Or else a cogged pulley hidden in an indefinite place. A lid the size of a florin interposes itself between his mouth and his stomach. He feels in his middle a rapidly revolving ball pulling at an incalculable number of threads tied to the surface of his skin. A shell envelops his head but leaves a part of his brain exposed. There are two small pieces of wood screwed onto his temples, etc. The temples play an important role in his suffering, both actual and imaginary. The arrow of love was shot not at his heart, he says, but into his temples. Again he writes to Milena:

You refer to my engagement and to other matters of the same kind; it was very simple, certainly; not the suffering but its effect. It was as if I had been spending my life in debauchery and suddenly they caught me in order to punish me; as if they had put my head in a vise, one jaw on the right temple, one jaw on the left temple. . . .

Thus his mind is the theater or rather the cinema of phantasmagoria which he faithfully records in his *Diaries*, without, for the most part, being astonished by it. He does, however, reach the point of revealing the shadow of madness over himself and of fearing it. He describes this fear of insanity particularly on December 25, 1915, January 16 and 22, 1922. He is also obsessed by thoughts of suicide, which always take the same form. "After which, I remained for an hour on the sofa thinking about Jumping-out-of-the-window." [March 8, 1912] A little later, "jumping out of the window" appears once more "as the only solution." And if he happens to think that marriage, perhaps, might be even better for him than suicide, besides permitting a favorable development of his vocation, he points out: "This, of course, is a conviction that I grasp at the moment when I am already, in a way, on the window sill." [August 15, 1913]

Later, in an absurd but comforting reverie, he connects this salvation through death with a none the less preserved life: "Jump out of the high window but fall on the rain-softened ground where the impact will not be mortal . . ." [July 6, 1916] In the same way, *he enjoys* (in imagination)

a suffering that causes him no pain and may pass at once.
[October 30, 1911]

We shall leave to a psychoanalyst the problem of drawing the dividing line here between reason and derangement, poetry and pathology. Be that as it may, it seems that something abnormal has entered into the acuteness of a vision which accumulates precise details recorded in a second. From this enlargement of reality is born a feeling of unreality, by which Kafka seems to be less disturbed than reassured, as if he felt more at home in the dream world. We find in his *Diaries* numerous accounts of dreams which are not without resemblance to reality as he describes it in his novels. We find numerous reveries, hypnagogic images, halfway between consciousness and sleep, that, without the least discontinuity, lead him into dreams that resemble life or a dematerialized life. One of his greatest needs is "to put to the test the solidity of the world." He has as much trouble in accepting his exclusion from his imaginary lives as in being concerned about his true existence: "This afternoon, before falling asleep—but I didn't sleep at all—I had the bust of a wax woman lying on me. . . ."

As a result, there is a constant threat of depersonalization. He *no longer knows what he is at this moment,* "whether I am indifferent, timid, young or old, insolent or devoted, whether my hands are before me or behind me, whether I am shivering with cold or feel warm, etc." The enumeration continues for a long time in this way until a "whether I am a Jew or a Christian," which is, indeed, the most amazing of doubts on his part. It is with relief that he begins to think, at another time, that the women who are walking behind him, one Sunday afternoon, can still see him enter a house with a hasty step: "There is nothing to indicate that this will last for long."

Haunted by obsessions, among which suicide, as we have seen, was not the least important, inhabited by monsters whose physical contact he seemed to feel, tormented even while awake by nightmares, sleeping little or poorly, experiencing a kind of panicky timidity in the presence of strangers (for him, every human being, and even he, himself, was a stranger), Kafka could only suffer, particularly from the work at which he earned a living. More than any other man, he felt the oppression of the permanent inanity of office life, the boredom, the constraint, of which millions of men are more or less consciously victims. For one part of his work, the source is the office. We have new proof of this in reading the *Letters to Milena:* "The office is not any old stupid institution (it is that, also, and superabundantly), but . . . it is related to the fantastic rather than to the stupid." The office is foreign to him to an absurd degree: "For me, the office—and it was the same way in primary school, at the lycée, at the university, in the family, in everything—the office is a human being, a living creature who looks at me." His letters are studded with sentences like this one: "There is another stranger at my office." Or: "A new interruption again; I shall no longer be able to write at the office."

Kafka belongs to the unfortunate breed whose qualities, in our society, cannot be converted into money. Feeling the breath of annihilation upon him, yet realizing his true value, he has to keep up appearances in a world that is indifferent when it is not openly hostile.

He assumes that there is only one effective occupation: that of writing. In the solid world, on the earth of men, "there is nothing else but literature." [*Diaries*] Anything that is not literature bores him and *he hates it.* "I feel myself disarmed and on the margin of everything. But the reassurance which the least literary work provides me is indubitable and marvelous." We find the best definition of his art in his *Diaries* for 1914: "The talent I have for describing my inner life, a life that is closely associated with the dream world..."

Literature appears to have been the only reason Kafka had for living, the only one over which, for a long time, he had any control. For years the vain yet oppressive duties of the office made it impossible for him to write except at night —and with all the more difficulty in that he experienced physical discomfort constantly and, if he slept badly during the night, would remain half-asleep for the rest of the time. ("... Last year I was not wide-awake more than five minutes...." [January 19, 1911]) None the less he devoted all his energies to the composition of works into which he put his only confidence. All of Kafka's complexes disappear as soon as his role is no longer that of a man but of a writer. Not that he is always, or even very often, satisfied with what he writes. But he knows he is on the right path. There and nowhere else is the road of hope for him (at least during the greater part of his life). He considers himself ugly. He discovers that he is unfit for all social activity. But as soon as he is writing and no matter what trouble this creative work costs him, everything brightens up, everything becomes simple: "I am terrified because I see that everything in me is ready for a poetic work, that this work would be a divine solution for me, a real entrée into life, while at the office I must, on account of some miserable paper work, rip a piece of flesh from the body capable of such happiness." [October 3, 1911] How many writers, obligated to such tasks, will recognize themselves in these lines. . . . Only a strong call allows us to surmount such ordeals—and that lassitude—in the evening.

It is curious to hear Kafka speak so severely about his indolence and fatigue at the very moment when he is actually negating them by the act of describing them—and writing. This man who was so simple was not afraid, however, to refer to his talent: "This evening, I felt myself once more filled with an anxiously restrained talent." [November 19, 1911] Truly, according to Max Brod, his genius. He did, at any rate, have a moment of weakness—if not necessarily of denial—when he forbade Brod to publish his manuscripts after his death. No doubt, he was at the moment in one of those states of depression, and, at the same time, of acute awareness, when what he had considered essential up to that time lost all its importance along with the rest. But he seems to have re-examined his decision. At least that is the way Max Brod interpreted the permission that Kafka gave him, shortly before his death, to publish four novelettes for which he chose the common title *Ein Hungerkünstler:* "Consideration of all these indications of a will turned toward life," writes Max Brod, "gave me the courage to attach no value to his prohibition to publish his writings after death, a prohibition, moreover, which he had written much earlier." [*Op. cit.*, p. 229] Although it is serious to disobey a dead friend, we cannot disapprove of this faithless trustee.

In the last years of his life, when, furthermore, he kept his diary more irregularly (to the point where there is only one page for 1923 and nothing for 1924, the year of his death), allusions to his writing occur less and less frequently in Kafka's notes. His despair in these last years was just as profound, but he dramatized it less and less, which does not

mean that he did not consider it tragic. Kafka seems to have
understood that only silence has the same dimension as death.
The author of "In the Penal Colony" never hoped for glory
from his books, but for salvation.

The first, chronologically, of Kafka's fictional fragments,
"Wedding Preparations in the Country" (1907-08), has been
published recently. These few pages, of a strange and powerful beauty, bear in visible fashion the germ, not only of the
author's entire work, but even of the groping works of his
more or less conscious disciples of today. With the single exception of this piece, it is in Kafka's *Diaries* that we find the
rough outlines of his works, the beginning of many broken-
off novelistic attempts, the source of his most cherished
myths, for example, the one about Justice (but who is judged,
by whom and why?) : "A call resounds ceaselessly in my ear:
may you come, invisible judgment!" [December 20, 1910]
"Joy and pain, guilt and innocence, like two hands clasped
in an unbreakable grip; it would be necessary to cut through
flesh, blood and bone to separate them." [December 8, 1919]
And if he commits a crime in a dream, "his happiness consists of this, that punishment is coming, and he is capable of
welcoming it freely, with such conviction and joy, the sight
of which should move the gods; and he experiences this emotion of the gods to the point of tears." [October 20, 1921]
Kafka is not unaware that a certain person is "infinitely
more innocent than he, there is no possible comparison on
this point." [January 22, 1922] In the famous "Letter to His
Father," written in 1919, which never reached the addressee,
he explains the feeling of guilt which is at the source of his
personal drama as well as of some literary renderings of it,

which he attempted more in order to unburden himself than as a man of letters. If we are to believe him, the crushing personality of his father and his father's system of education were partly responsible for his nervous deterioration. It is touching to feel how much Franz Kafka loved this man whom he believed he detested. He hopes in the end to make his relations with him not only normal and peaceful but affectionate. Kafka can only be assured of his presence in the world by being *against* his father, but he can imagine no repose or happiness *without* him.

For Milena to know more about his *occupations*, he adds a sketch to one of his letters. Four posts; two crossbars to which are attached the hands of the *offender;* two more bars for the feet. Once the wretch is tied thus, the bars are slowly drawn apart until the body of the victim bursts: "Against a column the inventor leans, his arms and legs crossed to give him a very important air as if he had discovered an original process, whereas he has merely copied the way a pork-butcher displays a disemboweled pig in his stall." Little work here for the psychoanalyst; Kafka is before us, like those mines with veins that can be exploited under the open sky.

It was not we, it was Kafka who underlined *offender.* Another key word of modern mythology. The second side of the diptych. On one side is the stranger; on the other, the guilty one. (It is not by chance that a book by Albert Camus is called *The Stranger,* a book by Georges Bataille *The Guilty One,* nor that Camus' hero is guilty at the same time that he is a stranger.) This notion of guilt, so important already in Dostoevski, has been laicized by Kafka, and our century remains obsessed with it. Whatever we do, and even if we do nothing, we are in a state of infraction. Franz Kafka feels he is responsible for Milena's insomnia (since she translated his books late into the night) so that he writes, with just enough irony to mask his anxiety which feeds on anything: "If a court tries the case, it will not bother with the fine points but simply establish the fact that I have deprived you of sleep. Of this I shall be found guilty and justly so." These references to a justice both legitimate and mysterious are frequent in the *Letters to Milena* as well as in the *Diaries:* "Who can say that he knows the secret thoughts of a judge?" Kafka is always ready "to bear witness against himself before courts of the highest instance."

If we are found guilty of crimes of which we are innocent, we are, nevertheless, convicted justly, for we have committed crimes of which our judges are ignorant. We are reduced to hypotheses about them in Kafka's case. It seems that he reproaches himself for certain of his sexual tendencies. Confiding one day, with less ambiguity than is customary for him, he writes to Milena that his body, after having been quiet for several years, is suddenly *racked unbearably with shooting pains of desire for a little abomination, an extremely specific bit of horror* (but just what he does not specify). Evil exists for Franz Kafka, and even original sin, which, he confesses, he understands better than anyone else. It is a kind of hell that permeates his works as well as his life.

Kafka has a secret: an obsession to which he refers in his diary without qualifying it. First, no doubt, because he knows it too well to need to describe it. (One writes a diary only to save from oblivion the best or most important things in one's life: what good would it do to record something which cannot be forgotten, which will never be forgotten?) And for this other reason, that whatever is written (or even simply professed) crystallizes what is uncertain, in some way gives it a material reality—and desperate people, so long as they do not kill themselves, never renounce hope completely. We find numerous traces of this secret in the *Diaries*. For example, on February 25, 1912:

Keep up the diary from today on! Write regularly! Don't give up! And even though deliverance should not come, I want to be worthy of it every instant. I spent the evening at the family table in complete indifference. . . . From time to time, I tried to become aware of my unhappiness; I hardly succeeded.

The preceding year, he had evoked "the creature of misfortune that I am." [January 12, 1911] He noted: "Should I thank or curse the fact that, in spite of all my misfortune, I can still experience love, an unearthly love but still for earthly beings?" [November 7, 1911] Later: "Complete knowledge of one's self. To be able to encompass the extent of one's capacities as the hand envelops a little ball. To resign oneself to the greatest failure as something familiar, in which one still remains flexible." [April 8, 1912] There are on the other hand innumerable references concerning his despair, his anguish, his timidity, his neurasthenia; we have already taken notice of them. "Miserable being that I am! . . . What distress!" [1913] This secret of Kafka's might have been placed side by side with that of Kierkegaard:

After I am gone there will not be found among my papers (therein lies my consolation) a single hint of what basically filled my life; there will not be found among my remains the text that explains everything, and which, for me, often makes events of enormous importance out of what the world would treat as bagatelles, and which, in my turn, I consider futile the moment I take away the secret note which is the key to it.

These lines are extracted from another diary: that of Soren Kierkegaard (1842–44). This secret may be common, no doubt it is analogous, and the temptation to attribute sexual origins to it is great. There was in both cases avoidance of marriage. Everyone will easily attribute a meaning to these half-confessions, and indeed so easily that one must be careful not to draw conclusions too quickly. And yet, Franz Kafka admits his *unhealthy sexuality*. He points out "the fact that he cannot have any mistresses, that he understands love about as much as he understands music." [January 2 and 3, 1912] He notes in July, 1916: "Never have I been intimate with a woman except in Zuckmantel. Then another time with a Swiss girl in Riva. The first one was a woman and I was ignorant, the second was a child and I was in the most complete confusion." When he describes Kafka's confidences about his experiences with women, Max Brod is able to recall, besides these two meetings at Zuckmantel and Riva, only a French teacher whom he mentioned from time to time and whose relations with Franz were already ancient history. [*Franz Kafka*, pp. 137–138] We read again in Kafka's *Diaries* for January 18, 1922:

What have you done with your gift of sex? They will say in the end that you made a mess of it and that will be all. But it could easily have been different. Certainly, a bagatelle was the deciding factor, and not even a recognizable bagatelle. What do you find surprising in that? It was the same in the great battles of history. The fate of bagatelles is decided by bagatelles.

The same word as that used by Kierkegaard, and used with the same seriousness: bagatelles. Bagatelles for an intimate massacre. The context and what we know of his life show that if Kafka was impotent, or, rather, feared impotence (which often amounts to the same thing), he was never completely so and he finally recovered from it.

Things are never very clear, or rather, they always are, for example; sex drives me, tortures me day and night; to satisfy it, I must overcome fear, shame, and no doubt unhappiness, too; but, on the other hand, I am sure that I should take advantage at once without fear or unhappiness of the first opportunity within my immediate reach that was offered willingly. According to what precedes, there remains the law which commands me not to conquer fear, etc. (but also not to play with the idea of triumph over fear), and to profit by the opportunity when it arises (but not to complain if it does not come). It is true, there is an intermediate step between "the act" and "the opportunity," the step where one instigates, where one attracts, the opportunity, a practice which, unfortunately, I have adopted not only in this case but in everything. From the point of view of the "law," an objection to this practice can hardly be raised, though the "instigation," especially when it is done with bad methods, suspiciously resembles "playing with the idea of triumph over fear," and in all that there is not the least trace of calm, frank fearlessness, capable of bearing anything. In spite of a "literal" agreement with the law, there is, precisely, something repugnant in it which it is absolutely essential to avoid. To avoid it, more restraint is necessary, and this I shall never achieve. [*Diaries*, January 18, 1922]

Love letters signed by Kafka exclude the possibility of any sentimental or spiritual release. Where most men would find happiness, or at any rate that sensual felicity and mental lethargy that pass for happiness, Kafka found only a more subtle and refined form of unhappiness. It was in 1920 that he fell in love with the young woman who produced the Czech version of his first "short prose pieces." Married, Milena was unfaithful, without, however, detaching herself from a husband whom she had ceased to love. It is difficult to measure her love for Kafka, since her own letters have been destroyed. The editor of the correspondence gives only a minimum of details about their liaison. Only allusions or barely decipherable clues in Kafka's letters offer us a few doubtful bits of information. The only sure point is that Franz and Milena saw each other rarely. Theirs was mainly a correspondence-relationship. This seems a particularly suitable form of love for Kafka. Not only did he make no effort to visit his friend more often (Prague is not so far away from Vienna), but he even seemed happy when, at the last moment, an incident made an anticipated meeting impossible. It was enough for him to know that in case of emergency he could go to Vienna: "That is my reserve, I live on it, as well as on your promise to come immediately if needed! That is why I shall not come now: instead of the certainty of those two days . . . I shall have the continuous possibility of them." They do, however, end by joining each other once more in a little town halfway between Prague and Vienna. Although no precise facts are given by the correspondents or their editors, this brief contact seems to have been fatal to their love. Franz and Milena soon stop seeing each other. He even insists that she stop writing to him. Milena, fantastic and fascinating, tortured, torturing, remains forever marked by this impossible love. Kafka transmitted his virus to her. In the dreams which he recounts to her and in which she plays an enigmatic role, it seems at times that we can divine a prefiguration of her fate. Loved, admired, adored, she was to die in the absurd, monstrous, Kafkaian universe of the concentration camps. As for him, he was already in jail, adjusting himself as best he could to "prison routine." We must realize that he was trying his best to live: an existence mid-way between the dream world and reality. His dreams have the peremptory acuteness of the true, his waking moments, the fluidity of dreams. It is difficult for us not to believe we are dealing with one of his nightmares when, with a laugh that hurts, he describes himself drifting down the Moldau, so thin, abandoned and alone in the boat where he is lying that a friend, noticing him from the top of a bridge, has the impression of witnessing the Last Judgment, "at the moment when the coffins are already open, but the dead do not as yet move."

In 1923, Franz met Dora Dymant, with whom he lived until his death. According to the testimony of Max Brod, this liaison *rid* him of his demons. When he went to visit the couple, Brod found Kafka leading *an idyllic life:* "I finally saw my friend in good spirits. His physical condition had become worse, it is true, but not yet bad enough to inspire serious fears." . . . "I was not the only one on whom Franz produced this impression of deliverance and revival. His good humor and his new assurance were apparent in his letters." [*Op. cit.,* pp. 228–229] But it was too late: death dwelt in him who (perhaps) had finally learned to live.

Kafka was the first to point out his kinship to Kierkegaard: "Today I received Kierkegaard's *Book of the Judge.* As I expected, his case is very similar to mine. In spite of essential differences, at least he is situated on the same side of the world. He supports me like a friend. . . ." [August 21, 1913] On August 27, 1916, he returns to the subject of this fraternity and the uselessness of the senseless comparisons between Kierkegaard and himself that he was wont to make. (He adds Flaubert and Franz Grillparzer.) We ought to keep in mind, especially, the note about beings *situated on the same side of the world.* There again, there in particular, the physical opens on the metaphysical. A whole race of writers from Kleist to Dostoevski lives on this other slope.

Kafka reminds us of a contemporary author who, indeed, belongs to his species, that of the sleepers (but it is the *other sleep*), of the wide-awake dreamers, of the Davids (fighting what Goliaths?) : Julien Green. The feeling of strangeness to himself and to the world (both are *strangers on earth*) ; the very special importance given to dreams and the tendency to judge them to be of greater truth than the so-called exterior reality—many other traits bring these two men close together. Kafka, however, lacks that palpable initiation into the supernatural which characterizes Julien Green. But he wrote nevertheless: "I live in this world as if I were absolutely sure of a second life. . . ." [February 21, 1911] And again (this could well be by Green) : "How I would like to explain the feeling of happiness which dwells within me from time to time, now, for example. . . ." [December 16, 1910]

This poor man, this great man, it is impossible to comment on his life and writings, it even seems difficult to quote him without seeming to betray him. We all have a little pathology in us, of course, and he more than many others. But for what do the overconfident diagnoses of reason count when the soul of a man is in the balance? An ephemeral soul, perhaps, but which exists, none the less, beyond time. An eternal soul, even if it does not live any longer than the body: eternity cannot be measured.

ANTONIN ARTAUD

AS IN THE CASE OF KAFKA, IT IS DIFFICULT IF NOT IMPOSSIBLE to evaluate the works of Artaud without reference to the man who created them. His poetry is almost intransmissible. It is not inexpressive, but rather it is expressive in the way that human cries can be. *Cry,* moreover, is the title of one of his very first poems. It was printed in the *Nouvelle Revue Française* of September 1, 1924, not for its poetic value, but because it happened to be quoted by Artaud himself in the course of one of his letters about his work of that time. Jacques Rivière had inserted these letters in his review in place of the works themselves, which he considered unpublishable.

When Artaud evokes the *men tortured by language* and names them (François Villon, Charles Baudelaire, Edgar Poe, Gérard de Nerval), he knows that he belongs to the same breed: the poets who *suffer their works*. Reproved, accursed, they *transude* rather than write. As far back as 1923, in the letters to Jacques Rivière, Antonin Artaud makes a diagnosis of the metaphysical illness with which he was afflicted. "I am suffering from a frightful malady of the mind. My thoughts evade me in every way possible. (It is a question of) a total absence, an actual loss." The few fragments which he submitted to the editor of the *n.r.f.* constitute "those remnants which he was able to win away from complete oblivion." Rivière's condemnation was for Artaud equivalent to denying him any sense of reality. If these passages do not succeed in *existing as literature*, their author will be deprived of his only claim to existence: "The whole problem of my thinking is at stake. For me it is a question of nothing less than knowing whether or not I have the right to continue to think, in verse or in prose."

Jacques Rivière replied that "the awkwardness and disconcerting strangeness" of his poetry did not preclude the possibility "that with a little patience he will reach the point of writing perfectly coherent and harmonious poems." Artaud describes his real problem, which will be the real problem throughout his life: *as a central crumbling of the soul, a kind of erosion of thought, essential and at the same time fugitive*. He is "a man who has had great mental suffering and who, by this token, has the right to speak." His weaknesses "have living roots, roots of anxiety."

There is something that is destroying my thinking, something that does not prevent me from being whatever I shall be able to be, but that leaves me, so to speak, in suspense. Something furtive which takes away the words *that I have found*, which diminishes the intensity of my mind, which, step by step, destroys in its substance the bulk of my thinking, which goes so far as to take away from me the memory of the figures of speech and devices by which one expresses oneself. . . .

His whole generation is suffering, Artaud indicates, from a "weakness that touches the very substance of what has been conventionally called the soul, and which is the emanation of our nerve forces coagulated around objects." In 1924 he wrote that Tristan Tzara, André Breton, and Pierre Reverdy showed symptoms of this sickness: "But in their case, their soul is not affected in a physiological way, nor is it deeply affected. It is only affected at all points where it touches upon something else, so that it is not affected anywhere *except in their thinking.*" They do not suffer, while the pain that afflicts him tortures him "not only in the mind, but in the everyday flesh": "This non-application to the object which is characteristic of all literature is in my case a non-application to life. I can truly say that I am not of this world and this is not simply an attitude of mind."

Jacques Rivière understood. Therefore, in the *n.r.f.,* in place of Artaud's poems he published the letters in which the poet comments on them, as well as his own replies. These are fine, intelligent and such as one could hope for from this man who was himself in a state of continual uneasiness and self-doubt. Two lines from Jacques Rivière show how far he entered into the drama of Artaud, a drama which is not so much of a period as of Man (but which, in this accursed poet, as in Kafka, is carried to a point of exemplary incandescence): "Proust described the *intermittences of the heart;* now one must describe the intermittences of human beings."

Antonin Artaud loses contact with his ego; it is continually in retreat and as though cut off from him. As he points out again to Rivière: "He is not completely himself, not as tall, thick or wide as he really is." His entire life will be spent chasing after his real self, trying to catch his double, in order to fuse with it and at last become only one being. Yes, Jacques Rivière understood Antonin Artaud as much as one could understand him at that time. But we, who know the sequel and the end of his life, give these letters of 1923–24 a significance which escaped not only Rivière but even Artaud. Fortunately for him, Artaud never believed himself to be incurable and regardless of how much his disorder became aggravated he never gave up all hope. If he submitted manuscripts to Rivière, it was in order to prove to himself "that he could still be something," and, above all, a writer: "This is my particular weakness and my *absurdity*, to want to write at any price and express myself."

Some of Artaud's work finally appeared in the December 1, 1925, issue of the *n.r.f.* (Jacques Rivière died at the beginning of the year and probably it was not he but Jean Paulhan who decided to publish it). These are no longer letters in which he explains that he wants to write and that it is his only hope of salvation, but actual literary works. These three fragments: *Positions de la chair, Manifeste en langage clair* and *Héloïse et Abélard,* bring us new proof of Artaud's permanent place in letters which was, once and for all, established from this time on. When he writes that "the Sense and Science of every thought is hidden in the nervous vitality of the bones," we recognize one of his fundamental convictions, and also that word *bones,* used in the Kafkaian sense. The same is true of *Correspondance de la momie,* which appeared in the *n.r.f.* in March, 1927:

. . . All this which makes of me a mummy of live flesh gives God an idea of the void in which I have been placed by the necessity of being.

... But from the top to the bottom of this pitted flesh, through this non-compact flesh, the undeveloped fire always circulates. The lucidity which hour after hour glows in its braziers is joined by life and its flowers.

Or, commenting on Jean de Boschère's *Marthe et l'Enragé,* in a note in the September 1st issue of the same year: "A marvelous flowering of mica trembles in the midst of the submarine beams of the subconscious come to light." But 1927 is the year of *Pèse-nerfs* (Nervometer), followed by *Fragments d'un journal d'enfer* (Fragments of a Diary in Hell), titles that are in themselves significant: "There is nothing in me, nothing in what makes up my personality, which was not produced by the existence of an evil *antedating* me, *antedating* my will." He is in *despair from solitude.* Drugs? Certainly. But they are the consequence, not the cause. To a woman whom he reproves for judging him sexually and not intellectually, he writes (still in *Pèse-nerfs*) :

I have only one more thing to tell you: that is, that I have always had this disorder of the mind, this crushed feeling in body and soul, this kind of contraction of all my nerves, at more or less closely spaced periods; and if you had seen me a few years ago, before I could even have been suspected of the practice for which you reproach me, you would no longer be surprised now at the reappearance of these phenomena. . . . Whatever the outcome, I can no longer count on you in my distress, since you refuse to take an interest in the most affected part of me: my soul. Besides, you have never judged me except on my exterior appearance, as all women do, as all idiots do, while it is my inner soul that is most destroyed, most ruined: and for that I cannot forgive you, for the two, unfortunately for me, do not always coincide.

I have spent a little time on these early writings to indicate that the deterioration of his mental state, which became more and more clear-cut, would subsequently overwhelm

Antonin Artaud without producing any essential modifica-
ation in the spiritual ordeal that he had experienced and
known for a long time. Even in his worst moments of aberration he would never lose sight of it. Insanity, if it was insanity, is, therefore, no explanation, even if it was the cause
of the intellectual perdition which the patient continually
describes. Artaud's dementia reveals the dementia of all
living men who think. It is the deflagration that leads to the
discovery of the explosive charge cautiously carried by all
of us. Thanks to this amplification what has escaped detec-
tion by being in a latent state becomes apparent. It is not so
much insanity as the impossibility of being, the horror of
essential solitude. "I live and was born with the unlimited
temptation of the human being: what shall I be, where am
I from, where shall I go and how?" [*Supplément au voyage
au pays des Tarahumaras* (Supplement to the Voyage to the
Land of the Tarahumaras)]. As he wrote in October, 1945,
from the asylum at Rodez, to Henri Parisot: "With me it is
the absolute or nothing, and that is what I have to say to
this world which has neither soul nor agar-agar." The
absolute or nothing. Such is the greatness of this man. For
most of us, the alternative is the same, but we turn our
attention, at no matter what price, from this fundamental
dilemma.

As far back as 1917 Antonin Artaud was mentally ill. At
that time he underwent a mystical crisis and experienced
violent nervous suffering. At the end of 1918 he entered a
Swiss rest home, where he remained for two years. Sent
to Paris by his parents, he stayed, to begin with, at Villejuif,
under the care of Dr. Toulouse. By 1921 he was considered
cured. But we have seen what he could write to Jacques
Rivière two years later. He was to be confined again in 1939

at Ville-Evrard, which he left in 1943 to be confined at Rodez under somewhat less unpleasant conditions until 1946 (two years before his death). A frightful calvary, because Antonin Artaud, though he thought and acted at times like an insane person, did not feel more at odds with himself then than when he was at liberty. He never ceased to be conscious of his difference, if not of his illness, and he lived as well—or rather as badly (but without danger to others)— free as incarcerated. On the one hand, he knew more about his sickness than the psychiatrists who treated him. On the other hand, he was not unaware that in its essence this illness was not exclusively his. This was something that the doctors, distracted by their specialty from the true drama of humanity, forgot.

And human beings can stammer in vain that things are as they are, and that there is nothing further to seek. I see, indeed, that they have lost their bearings and that for a long time *they have no longer known what they were saying*, for they no longer know where they used to go in search of the states of mind with which they can stretch out upon the flow of ideas and from which they get words with which to speak.

If he often speaks of madness—his madness—it is as a rational person. Comparing the European to the Tarahumara, he notes that the European, in contrast to the latter, would never accept the possibility "that what he has felt and perceived in his body, that the emotion which has shaken him, that the strange idea which has just stirred him with its beauty, was not his own but that of another person who has felt and experienced all this through his body; otherwise he would believe himself to be mad and people would be tempted to say that he had become a lunatic." [*Le Rite de peyotl* (The Peyote Rite)]

He insists that peyote does not *make one take dreams for reality,* nor does it "confuse true images and emotions with perceptions borrowed from depths that are fleeting, un-nurtured, not yet ripe, not yet raised from the hallucinations of the subconscious." If he defends himself in this way it is because he is aware that his mind may be accused of wander-ing. By convincing his contradictors that peyote does not affect the essence of thinking, he is also trying to justify those of his hallucinations that are due to no drug other than that borne by his sick blood. "I also," he points out, "had false sensations and perceptions and I believed in them. But since then I have felt my energy and clarity return. [*Le Rite du peyotl*] In the *Lettres de Rodez,* we see him con-stantly trying to get back his bearings, even when he seems to be most astray. In the letter of October 6, 1945, for ex-ample, he begins in a rational way, only to fall back into delirium. But by the third page he emerges from the shadows. "I need poetry in order to live, and I want to have it around me. And I do not concede that the poet in me was locked up in an insane asylum because he wanted to achieve poetry in its natural state." After this, he immediately sinks again: "I concede even less that groups of bewitchers, made up of the entire population of Paris, taking turns endlessly night and day, place themselves in the streets and boulevards at certain hours that they have agreed and decided upon in advance in order to cast upon me floods of hatred. . . ."

In almost all of his last works Antonin Artaud tries desperately to *prove* the existence and reality of these spells. To Henri Parisot he points out: "I want the last friends that I may have on this earth and who are my last readers, to be enlightened, and to understand that I was never mad, or ill, and that my incarceration is the result of a frightful occult plot in which all sects of the *initiated*, Christians, Catholics, Mohammedans, Jews, Buddhists, Brahmans, plus the lamas of the Tibetan monasteries, have participated." Warnings, reproofs, supplications, of the same order are numerous. One could cite several dozen. In his lecture at the Vieux Colombier on January 13, 1947, he elaborates: "At Rodez, it was never possible for me to mention the word 'spell' in front of Dr. Ferdière without immediately being accused of being delirious." Artaud himself reports this pathetic dialogue in which he calls upon the most subtle resources of dialectics to defend his hallucinations:

—Come, come, Monsieur Artaud, I think your delirium is taking hold of you again.
—What do you mean, my delirium? I am citing facts and I'll show you proof.
—But that's it, that's it exactly, delirium with stubbornness. Well, I am going to recommend a series of electric shocks for you and write to your friend Jean Paulhan that I am going to give you shock treatments again.
—But, in short, I am not the only writer to have spoken about witchcraft, and Huysmans in *Là-bas*——
—Huysmans was crazy, like you, and all those who believed in the afterlife were crazy; look at Nietzsche and Gérard de Nerval. As for the spells, never has there been scientific proof of a spell, and since you are obstinate about it you will never leave this house and will remain confined throughout your life.

One might say that Artaud is exhibiting the logic of paranoia. It is so forceful, however, that the psychiatrist speaks to him as to a sane man, trying in turn to convince Artaud and threatening him with sanctions as though he were a responsible person. In this type of illness the patient is healthy in everything that does not touch on his particular mania. Hence the alternating lucidity and delirium. After his lecture at the Vieux Colombier, Antonin Artaud wrote to Maurice Saillet: "I noticed particularly (in your review in *Combat*) the sentence concerning enchantments where you say that my revelations about them elicited no interest. I noticed it all the more since, like you, I was aware that they had indeed fallen upon empty air. However, the facts that I cited should have been enough to arouse a whole hallful of spectators . . ."

That Artaud's mind was damaged, no one can doubt. His last writings are for the most part devoid of significance or even reduced to onomatopeia. He even goes so far as to think he is Jesus Christ. Certainly there must have been physical causes for his aberration, but Artaud always realized that his illness was above all (like Kafka's) metaphysical in nature. He never stopped evoking God: sometimes to adore him, more often to blaspheme him, but, with or without the capital letter, God was always there. Artaud felt excluded from a reality which he happened to believe was supernatural. As far back as 1927 he exclaimed: "The most diseased part of me: my soul."

At one period, Antonin Artaud was converted to Catholicism. Later, he could not find enough insults, sarcasm, and obscenity with which to dissociate himself from what he considered thereafter to be a new, particularly subtle and noxious, form of enchantment. He points out in a postscript: "I wrote the *Rite du peyotl* in a state of conversion, with a hundred and fifty or two hundred hosts already in my body; these were the cause of my occasional delirium about Christ and the cross of Jesus Christ. Nothing now seems to me more ominous and ill-fated than the stratifying and limiting sign of the cross, etc." It was for this reason that, in September, 1945, Antonin Artaud asked Henri Parisot to exclude from the *Pays des Tarahumaras* the *Supplément au voyage* "in which I was imbecile enough to say that I had been converted to Jesus Christ, whereas the Christ is what I have always abominated most. This conversion was only the result of a frightful enchantment. At Rodez it made me swallow a fearful number of hosts disguised as communion; these were supposed to keep me for as long as possible, and, if possible, eternally, inside a being which is not my own." This *Supplément au voyage au pays des Tarahumaras* was, therefore, sacrificed in the original edition published by *Fontaine* in 1945. Its disavowal does not, however, make it not worth quoting from.

Antonin Artaud begins by evoking the demons who are attacking him, "this being that I constantly see faltering before my eyes as long as God has not placed his key in my heart. One sees God when one wants to, and to see God is not to be satisfied with the little enclave of terrestrial sensations. . . . One day I was far from God but never had I also felt so far away from my own self, and I saw that without God there is neither identity nor being, and that the man who still believes he is living will never again be able to understand himself." In the Ciguri of the Tarahumaras, *he could not but recognize Jesus Christ.* A letter to Henri Parisot of December 10, 1942, states: "I shall pray especially to Jesus Christ about this, for my whole Voyage to Mexico concerns Him, and it is He, the Word of God, whom the Tarahumaras adore, as I was able to observe in the rite of the *Tutuguri* which takes place at sunrise." As for the *Supplément*, it concludes: "And it is this God of Eternal Charity whom I went and found the following year among the Icelanders." This refers to another trip, his last, about which he makes these comments in a letter to Jean-Louis Barrault dated October, 1943:

The thought which permitted me to support my ordeals without flinching: God. I came back to Him in Dublin in September, 1937, and it was there that I took confession and communion after twenty years of estrangement from the Church and several years of atheism and blasphemy with which all my works are studded. This means that, except for my correspondence with Rivière, the "Théatre et son double" and "Nouvelles Révélations de l'Etre," I disavow all my written works and I shall have them all destroyed.

According to this passage, he apparently kept his faith until 1917 (the period of his first mental disturbance), then reverted to it again from 1937 to 1944. By what right, then, should we accept his denunciation of his Christian rather than his blasphemous works?

Whether he refers to a metaphysical system or to a system of magic, it is obvious that Antonin Artaud is interpreting them according to his own concepts. No doubt this is what all believers do. As objective observers, however, we cannot give preference to one or other of these spiritual positions. Artaud's interpretative approach is noticeable, for example, in his ideas concerning mescaline. He assures us in the *Rite du peyotl* that "Mystics must pass through similar states before attaining supreme illumination." And in the *Supplément au voyage:* "It is then that the peyote given by Jesus Christ intervenes. It takes the soul from behind and sets it in the eternal light, such as comes from the Spirit on high. . . ." A note written after the *Rite* pokes fun at this interpretation: "As for peyote, it does not lend itself to these offensive spiritual assimilations, for MYSTICISM has never been anything but a copulation of a very learned and very refined *tartufferie* against which peyote thoroughly protests, for with it MAN is alone, desperately rattling the music of his skeleton, without father, mother, family, love of god or society." But in the *Supplément* he wrote what seems incontestable, whether or not it is considered from the Christian point of view: *"I had certainly never experienced anything of God* (thanks to peyote), *for it is not by means of an experimental physical test that one reaches the Godhead. . . ."*

Here the madman Artaud seems more rational than the wise Aldous Huxley, according to whom mescaline enables one *to experience the heights of contemplation.*

Whether Artaud recognizes himself as a Christian or not, whether he reveres Christ or blasphemes him, seems less important to me than to the pseudo-rebels of the *nth* surrealist generation who go into a trance at the very name of Jesus while they feel respect for the bloodiest beliefs of the Aztecs or the Tarahumara rites. Such sensitivity surprises observers who consider themselves unconnected with any form of supernaturalism. It is the credulity of these pseudo-atheists that is impressive. A subconscious nostalgia for the faith causes them to disown Christianity the better to abandon themselves to a metaphysical appeal whose heterodox, exotic, and indeterminate form reassures them. As for me, it makes no difference whether this poet, who is visibly *inspired,* claims this or that religion. Artaud went to Christ just as he went to Ciguri. It was not by chance that he happened to confuse them. It would be unfair to use this as an argument in favor of the conception of Artaud as a Christian. But it is also just as unacceptable to overlook the date of his conversion, as has been done too often, and only remember his blasphemies and *other* beliefs. What really matters is not Artaud the Christian, nor Artaud the magician, nor Artaud planning to go "the way of the Himalayas" to be initiated into new mysteries. No, what is important is Artaud at constant and direct grips with metaphysics.

In one of his letters from Rodez, Antonin Artaud admits that, above all, he went to seek in Mexico a race that would follow his ideas. This indicates that he, too, was only looking for what he had already found. Very much along the same lines is this declaration from a letter of April 2, 1926: "I plan to leave Mexico City shortly for the interior of Mexico. I am leaving in search of the impossible. We shall see whether I shall find it." In the *Rite du peyotl* he carried this search for the impossible toward an objective that was scarcely more modest: "I told him (the Priest) also that I had not come to the Tarahumaras out of simple curiosity but to rediscover a Truth, conserved by his Race, which has eluded the European world." His commentary, in the *Supplément au voyage*, changes nothing essential in this: "Thus it was that, driving on toward God, I rediscovered the Tarahumaras."

Antonin Artaud spoke a great deal also about good and evil. He never ceased to know what was good and what was evil. Here again citations abound. He writes that "Evil is in the order of things and man can no longer feel pure." He adds that "the struggle between Good and Evil is not yet finished. In order for the reign of God to arrive on earth, we must be chaste." These notes are from Rodez, but the same theme is found again after his renunciation of Christianity in the poems written during the last months of his life, published by the review *84*. In them, Artaud denounces "the hideous world of lubricity and the obscene proposition of a world without judgment or ethics. . . . This true story of mine is shocking. It is the story of a man who wanted to be good and pure but nobody wanted him, because men can can never get along with anything but impurity, impiety, injustice and assassination. It is very difficult to be pure, but when one must be pure in the face of general ill will that does everything it can to keep one in a state of evil, as if by force, it becomes a desperately difficult chore." On this point the judgment of Arthur Adamov appears definitive and cannot be questioned even by our pious fanatics of impiety. We find it in the same issue of the review *84*: "He believed in enchantments, and in a literal way. But I have reason to think that in large measure Antonin Artaud's belief in enchantments was born from an impossibility, from a refusal to admit the existence of evil in the world, and I would say almost from too great a love."

There is nothing to add, except perhaps to quote the Dominican, Father Laval: "In short, here is the true language of a man who is suffering."

HENRY
MILLER

IT IS RARE FOR HENRY MILLER NOT TO BE SPEAKING ABOUT himself. Even in a short work on a precise and limited subject, such as *A Devil in Paradise,* he is unable to avoid wandering into digressions which remind us that the only theme dear to this author is his own person, his obsessions, his secrets. A person who always ends by slipping into the foreground and by imposing on us the fantasies of his personal delirium. An ordered delirium, worked into shape, and turning into wisdom. Images caught in the trap of writing without losing any of their abundance but with their noxiousness removed, thanks to this planned metamorphosis. There are many contemporary writers for whom literature is a personal therapy. Henry Miller is one of those who owe their health to their works.

Thus a new dimension is added to literature. The objective of a whole life, it is in the end the life's reward and tends to negate itself in the process, becoming *aliterature,* that is, literature purified of all that is hypocrisy, untruth, pretension, verbal inflation. In the *Tropic of Capricorn* the literary vocation is described by the young Miller:

I found that what I had desired all my life was not to live—if what others are doing is called living—but to express myself. I realized that I had never had the least interest in living, but only in what I am doing now, something that is parallel to life, of it at the same time, and beyond it. What is true interests me scarcely at all, nor even what is real; I am interested only in what I imagine, in what I stifle every day in order to live. Whether I die today or tomorrow is of no importance to me, never has been, but that today even, after years of effort, I cannot say what I think and feel—that bothers me, that rankles. From childhood on I can see myself on the track of this specter, enjoying nothing, desiring nothing but this power, this ability. Everything else is a lie—everything I ever did or said which did not bear upon this. And that is pretty much the greater part of my life.

Another book, *Plexus,* tells us about his difficult and long literary apprenticeship. Until his arrival in Paris, only three short pieces had been published in the United States over Miller's signature: the first by a magazine specializing in the problems of colored people; the second in a friend's review which had only one issue; the third in a periodical that was scarcely more substantial.

In the beginning Henry Miller was possessed by so violent a desire to write that it was actually difficult for him to try to express himself: "The amount of physical energy that I had was unbelievable. I tired myself out in preparations. It was impossible for me to sit down quietly and simply let the flood loose; I was dancing inside." [*Plexus*] Letters were easy, he wrote endless ones; for lectures the wellspring seemed still more abundant. This was his double point of departure.

He noticed that no problem of form arose while he was carrying on his correspondence. Friends who had confidence in his still undeveloped talent saw the writer in him even before he had written anything, and advised him to give free rein to his inspiration, as he did when improvising his prodigious monologues. "Listen, sometimes when I hear you talk, I say: If only that guy would write down what he says! Boy, you'd be good enough to write a book which would make Dreiser want to hang himself." [*Tropic of Capricorn*]

Henry Miller quotes in *Plexus* this sentence from Louis Lambert: "I feel within me a life so luminous that it could animate a world, and I feel myself locked up in some kind of mineral." This statement seems to coincide exactly with what for a long time was his own state of mind. But the mineral did finally explode, forming with each of its fiery bursts those incandescent books where the best and the worst are so close to each other that they cannot be distinguished, much less dissociated. The author of *The Tropics* and *The Rosy Crucifixion* defies aesthetic evaluation. Questions of taste and of standards cannot be asked with regard to him. One accepts or rejects him as a whole: from a literary point of view his work is neither good nor bad, it exists. And its presence is crushing.

No reader ought to contest the legitimacy of the sexual lyricism of a great part of his creative work, an obscenity so powerful that it consumes itself in order to attain a kind of absolute purity. One reason for this is that first of all, we cannot, without being hypocritical, take exception to the description of a reality familiar enough in our private lives. Furthermore, Miller paid very dearly for the right to express himself in the way that he found best and most suitable for what he had to say. "I made all the mistakes that a man can possibly make and I paid the price for them," he says in *A Devil in Paradise,* where he points out that the privations which he suffered were endured through his own choosing. At thirty-three, he vowed never to work any more for anyone. "Regular work is all right for other guys—I would have no part of it. I had talent and I would cultivate it. I would be a writer or starve." [*Plexus*]

Henry Miller was a writer, but he starved.

When he was en route to Dijon, where, in a difficult period of his life, a teacher's job awaited him, Henry Miller evoked "those bitter and humiliating moments when asking for a piece of bread makes you feel lower than a worm. With my belly empty and my head clear, I could still feel the burning pain of those old-time insults and affronts." And not only in New York, the place in the world where he suffered most: "I wandered throughout the whole United States and even into Canada and Mexico. Same story everywhere. If you want bread, you must get into harness, you must walk in the chain gang." [*Tropic of Cancer*] In America, *when he sank, he touched bottom.* [*Souvenir Souvenirs*] In New York he took the lowliest jobs, which he left partly out of hatred for restraint, but especially to obey the dictates of his only vocation: writing. "Soon, I begged in the streets, furtively, in the evening, in the very neighborhood of my own house. Soon, I was standing in front of restaurant windows, looking at good things to eat with envy and despair. Soon I would be thanking the newsboys for the few cents they would give me to get a cup of coffee and a hot dog." [*Plexus*] Miller doesn't like New York, "the most horrible place on God's earth": "No matter how many times I escape, I am brought back like a runaway slave, each time detesting it, loathing it more and more." [Preface to the *Air-conditioned Nightmare*]

On the other hand, what nostalgia for Paris, always! We find it in *A Devil in Paradise*, where, as in so many other books of his, the very names of Paris streets set him dreaming. In this same work, he sees himself once more at the corner of Broadway and 42nd Street on an icy evening, the rain lashing his face: "Scrutinizing the passing crowd, trying to find a friendly face, a fugitive expression to assure me that I would not encounter a rebuff or a bit of spit by way of charity." And complaining about his friend Moricand: "Never did he have to go into the streets and beg. When he begged, it was with an elegant hand on fine writing paper." Besides, "he wasn't adaptable or supple enough to beg," this "indigent too proud to beg openly, but capable of bleeding a friend white." The boundary was always the same, hunger: a dividing line between men separated forever. It seems, however, that Moricand had experienced hunger too.

Transparently christened Téricand in the French edition of *A Devil in Paradise*, Conrad Moricand was to die in wretched poverty in Paris in 1954, shortly after his return from California where Henry Miller had given him shelter. The story of this invitation is told, with powerful humor shaded with touches of seriousness, in *A Devil in Paradise*. Miller had met Moricand in Paris in 1936. In the restaurant where he was invited to dinner, "his way of looking at the menu immediately gave him away as a busybody." An inexhaustible talker, as soon as the conversation turned to his specialty, the occult sciences, "he seemed somber, didactic, obstinate in his opinions, self-centered. His whole being was impregnated with a kind of fatalism." What immediately won Henry Miller over was that his new friend "was not only an astrologer and a learned imbiber of hermetic philosophy, but also an occultist." This "incurable dandy leading the life of a hobo" liked to believe, Miller tells us, "that there existed a connection between Moricand and Mohican. In his moments of chagrin, his expression had something slightly comic, as if he had consciously identified himself with the *Last of the Mohicans*."

That *A Devil in Paradise* is a more important book than was thought at first has been confirmed. It would not surprise me if, in painting the strange figure of Conrad Moricand, Henry Miller wanted to draw a caricature of himself. If this is so, he may not always have been aware of the resemblance between them.

After having invited Moricand, and having borrowed the money for the trip (a debt that was difficult for him to repay) ; after having welcomed him, taken him in, lodged and fed him; after having for a long while put up with the annoyance caused by the exigencies of his guest: his manias, illnesses and obsessions; after having found a way, without causing a rupture in their relations, for his guest to live elsewhere in the best possible conditions (but Moricand objected to any reasonable solution), the day came when Miller could stand it no more. Moricand showed such ill will toward helping the man who was helping him, that Miller, embittered, not only stopped his food but refused to hear anything more about him. It is true that Moricand had gone as far as blackmail, threatening Miller "if he wouldn't give in, to notify the authorities about the scandal his works had caused in France":

That wretch Téricand! Twisting things so! Presenting them, even if only to himself, as though by promising to take care of him, I had obligated myself to keep him in a hotel, give him an allowance to go to bars, theaters, to travel about by taxi. And if that weren't enough, to deposit a thousand dollars in his name in Paris. All that because Monsieur Téricand refused to become poor again! As if such an eventuality depended on our good pleasure!

Except for the sordid details which make Moricand's attitude toward Miller so distasteful, it is curious to recall a scene from *Tropic of Cancer* in which the roles are reversed. Like Moricand, Miller is put up by a friend; like him he is sick—and no less easy to take care of; tenacious, too, and obstinate, even while realizing that he is a nuisance: Kruger, his host, is an artist who is preparing an exhibit in the same studio where Miller has just become sick ("the excessively rich diet was having its effect") :

Had I been able to get on my feet, I know he would have walloped me and kicked me out. But I was laid low and sick as a dog. He tried to get me out of bed with kind words. . . . I knew that I was going to make him mad. People can't look at pictures and statues enthusiastically while a man is croaking before their eyes. Kruger seriously thought I was going to die. So did I. That is why, although I felt guilty, I couldn't raise an ounce of enthusiasm when he offered to get an ambulance and ship me to the American Hospital. . . . I refused to let him call the hospital. I refused to let him call the doctor. I refused everything!

In anger Kruger dressed the protesting Miller by force, took him to a hotel and abandoned him. Miller, when he came to his senses at last (certainly more friendly in his extremity than poor Moricand), assured him that he understood the situation and bore his friend no ill will.

Henry Miller is fully aware of the fact that no matter how much he follows the traces of his former I's, and writes, writes, writes indefinitely about the past that is still present within him, he will never come to the end of what his life has taught him. "No man can hope to live long enough to complete the journey through these events, these depthless experiences, through the medium of words," he writes in *A Devil in Paradise*. And he adds, a propos of those who, like him, were born under the sign of Capricorn:

They never forget anything. Their memory is fantastic. Not only do they remember their personal human tribulations, but prehuman and subhuman ones as well. They can slither back into their protoplasmic slime with the ease of eels in a vase. They keep the memory of the high spheres, of seraphic states, as if they had known long periods of freedom from earthly slavery, as if they were familiar with the language of the seraphim itself. . . . Their attitude is perpetually that of the man, who, casting a last look about, bids a final good-bye to earthly things.

"I have no problems," we read elsewhere in this book, "or else they are of a cosmic order. I am at peace with myself . . . and with the world." He thinks that "peace and joy are within everyone's reach." This philosophy seems simple only, perhaps, because truth is simple. We find it over and over again, in each of his books. "The only difference between the man of Adam's Age and the Present is that the former was destined for Paradise while the other must create it . . . Our essential being is similar to that of God. I say there is no limit to thought or actions. I say we are one, and not several, . . ." Miller, whose optimism is utopian, believes that it is potentially and effectively within the power of man to eliminate "war, sickness, old age, and probably death, too."

Henry Miller did not succeed in producing a masterpiece at first try. But in telling his own story, he found his tone, his rhythm. He gave us first some fragments of his life (*Tropic of Cancer, Tropic of Capricorn*), then, after some fictional essays, undertook the major work of his life. This was, is, and will be *The Rosy Crucifixion,* of which we still know only *Plexus,* the first of the two completed volumes (there will be three) ; the second volume, *Sexus,* has been banned.

He shows himself, in *Plexus,* transformed into *an enormous eye* to which no detail of reality is insignificant. The most common objects are transfigured. "From the moment one pays continuous attention to everything, even a simple blade of grass, everything becomes a world in itself, mysterious, imposing, unspeakably magnified." Yet it is the unspeakable that must be spoken. So, in his youth, Henry Miller "used to read faces, gestures, bearings, architecture, streets, passions, crimes. Everything, yes, everything was noted, analyzed, compared and described—for future use":

Studying an object, a fact, a façade, I would study them in the manner in which they would later be recorded in a book, including the adjectives, adverbs, prepositions, parentheses, what not. Even before I had sketched the plan of my first book, my mind swarmed with hundreds of characters. I was a walking, talking book, an encyclopedic compendium which never stopped swelling, like a malignant tumor.

If making love seems to him the closest, most efficacious, maddest and most reasonable way to embrace the universe, it is not the only approach possible for him. What is (mistakenly) called his obscenity is, as anyone who has read him attentively knows, only one aspect of his work.

Henry Miller can describe himself as part of the world; he is part of it.

MICHEL LEIRIS

MICHEL LEIRIS DESCRIBED HIMSELF IN *L'Age d'homme* (The Age of Man) as "a specialist, a maniac for confession." He thought he had to specify in the course of the same work that "if confession has an irresistible attraction for him, it is as a vehicle of humiliation, shame and exhibitionism." If confession appears so fascinating to the author of *La Règle du jeu* (Rule of the Game) it is, as he noted in the first volume, *Biffures* (Deletions), because he cannot bear to be judged for what he is not:

Like the lover anxious to be loved only "for himself," it is myself such as I am—and not as a stranger—that I wish to be accepted. In no way would it help to use counterfeit money in settling this account, in no way would it help to short-change anyone: I shall literally have to *pay with my person* if I conclude this bargain, which is a trade with myself as much as a transaction with others.

From book to book (I was going to say: from mirror to mirror—but never did Narcissus look at himself with less self-satisfaction) Michel Leiris probes his face and his whole physical appearance. The baldness with which he was threatened at the age of thirty-four, when he was writing the first pages of *L'Age d'homme,* reappears, as was foreseeable, in one of the last pages of his most recent work, *Fourbis.* Here also he describes the inflammation of the eyelids mentioned in the first portrait. Michel Leiris admits in several places in his works that he attaches a certain importance to the way he dresses. A concern for elegance which reached the point of coquetry in his youth is preserved today only in the form of an indispensable correctness. The reason for this fastidiousness in clothing is a form of self-defense. For Leiris it is not so much a matter of being handsome as of overcoming the weakness and ugliness of which he suspects himself. In *Aurora,* written at thirty, an imaginative work scintillating with personal avowals, we find the following revelation: "I looked on my own body only with disgust; I tried all possible ways of giving it a granitelike aspect, and often I remained motionless, for hours on end, thinking that thereby I could bring myself in some measure to be a statue."

What is important to Michel Leiris is not his body but what, without any metaphysical implication, we may call his soul. He is sensitive about his outer appearance only in so far as it betrays his inner disposition. Thus, for example, the clumsiness he so often attributes to his limbs "is only his lack of decision translated into physical terms." In *L'Age d'homme* as in the two volumes of *La Règle du jeu,* which recently appeared (and already, although to a lesser degree, in *L'Afrique fantôme* [Phantom Africa], we find innumerable observations relative to the author's character (he would say rather his lack of character).

Attaching the greatest value to *precise biographical references,* Michel Leiris permits himself no infraction of the absolute rule of perfection which was to remain his model. He is sorry to be "an execrable swimmer, a pitiful horseman, a nonexistent driver, and totally helpless when it comes to fist-fighting." Since he wants to make an honest balance sheet, he credits himself with being able to ride a bicycle, which constitutes, he points out "only a slim scrap of consolation." We should not allow ourselves to smile here except with a friendliness that does not consider anything ridiculous. Risking the insults of an irony as facile as it is uncomprehending is one of the dangers that Michel Leiris knowingly runs. His object is to recount everything that concerns him, beginning with what is ridiculous to those who only go by appearances.

Even the most normal taste, the taste for comfort, he exposes in himself in order to find fault with it, reproaching himself, for example, "for lazily abandoning to the bullfight enthusiasts of more modest means the seats where one broils in the sun, in order to relax, like a sybarite, in those which are in the shade." Michel Leiris comes back twice to this modest detail about his life as an *aficionado.* But he had more serious complaints to make about himself on this score. We know the importance of bullfights in the personal mythology of the author of the *Miroir de la tauromachie* (Mirror of Tauromachy) and especially of *De la Littérature considerée comme une tauromachie.* In the latter work he states that for him it is a matter of "baring certain obsessions of a sentimental or sexual order, confessing publicly certain deficiencies or acts of cowardice which make him feel most ashamed in order to introduce at least the shadow of a bull's horn into a literary work," thus depriving it, as far as possible, of its harmlessness. Michel Leiris informs us in *Fourbis* that he ended by "liquidating" not so much his interest in *corridas* as his literary exploitation of them:

What is repugnant to me now is not the thing itself (with its undeniable foundation of barbarousness in attractive trappings) but my own attitude toward this thing: appreciating as a dilettante a spectacle based on death and courage, when I myself am so uneasy about death and so little courageous.

There remains the real courage which he demonstrates above all by speaking about his cowardice. What he has the courage to call *cowardice*, a word we all fear when it comes to applying it to ourselves, is one of Michel Leiris's deepest obsessions. He sees the germ of it in the lack of energy he displayed, as a child, in the gymnasium where he was obliged to go every week. There he "let himself slide down a slope of sluggishness, stepping away at first from this dizzy exercise or that jump which would have called for too much effort, then going from default to default, ending by hiding from everything that demanded that his body be put to the test." Thus *he let a kind of impotence take root in his innermost being,* thus *he sank into a state of hopeless inadequacy as far as matters of physique and courage were concerned.*

From the first pages of *L'Age d'homme,* Michel Leiris calls himself "crushed by shame, feeling his whole being corrupted by this incurable cowardice." This *fear of life* made psychoanalytic treatment necessary and here the idea of writing *L'Age d'homme* was born. He exposed with as little complacence as reticence the various aspects of his disturbance. Childhood fears still dominated him, "analogous to those of a nation perpetually prey to superstitious terrors and in the power of cruel and somber mysteries." The impression that all pleasures must be paid for, especially those of love; simultaneous search for and fear of the different forms in which "suffering, failure, expiation, punishment" may be clothed. These, among many others, are some of the themes in *L'Age d'homme:*

I always behave like a kind of "accursed man" whose punishment pursues him eternally, who suffers because of it but who wishes nothing so much as to push to its peak this cursedness, an attitude from which I have for a long time derived acute though austere joy, eroticism for me being necessarily conjoined with torment, ignominy, and, even more, terror.

Similar confessions are found in *Biffures* where he denounces "his anxieties, his narcissism, his manias"; complacency "in the padded heedlessness of an egotistic solitude"; "weakness of character going hand in hand with pusillanimity in the practice of words"; "the same stage-fright panic when facing words to be linked as before an act to be accomplished. Always beating around the bush. Wavering. Shifting. Evading." And in *Fourbis:*

Being as stingy about myself as a miser could be about his pennies; bound by fear; reticent in love (perhaps on account of this fear of having to pay with my body which also causes me to shrink from the idea of grief); wanting to play the part of the *torero,* but without ever facing a real bull, and the part of Don Juan, without conquests or defying the Commander. . . .

Let us go no further in this inventory. The disadvantage presented by this genre of authors is that they say much more about themselves than their exegete can repeat if he does not want to take advantage of the ammunition they have provided. There is no need to read very much of Michel Leiris in order to come up with a diagnosis. "If modern ex-

plorers of the subconscious," he writes in *L'Age d'homme,*
"speak (in connection with me) about Oedipus, castration,
guilt feelings, narcissism, I do not think that it helps a great
deal as far as the essential part of the problem is concerned
(which remains, according to my way of thinking, related
to the problem of death and to the apprehension of oblivion
and so relates to metaphysics)." Perhaps, it would have
been better to speak of sadism and masochism (examples
abound in the aforementioned book) but what difference
does it make? The real question lies elsewhere.

Death haunts Michel Leiris. He returns to it ceaselessly.
L'Age d'homme opens with an evocation of it; a long chapter
of *Fourbis* is dedicated to it. As he notes in *Biffures,* it is
"the haunting of time and the obsession of decrepitude"
that are at the source of his literary attempts, which aim
at nothing less than the erection *of his own statue.* A statue
that resembles the model, that does not cheat about its de-
fects, but by the very fact that it solidifies and immobilizes
them in a work of art, is a relative guarantee against annihilation and oblivion. *Overwhelmed as he is by fear of
death,* Leiris writes "to compose a veneer of beauty to hide
from himself the horror of living." From the time that he
depended on poetry alone to express and save himself, he
held on to the conviction that "through the lyrical use of
words man has the power of transmuting all." (*Transmute*
is one of the words that for a long time he preferred to all
others.) The qualifying adjective *lyric* is no longer necessary
when he "tries to adopt autobiography as the sole means of
expression." By attacking "this rather special layer of memories which he undertakes to prospect," Michel Leiris hopes
to make a quasi-scientific use of literature. Hence "his almost maniacal interest in minute and not easily verifiable

facts resulting from what goes on in his innermost self."
Hence his patient, somewhat monotonous, and often seemingly pathological way of *churning himself up.*

The essence for Michel Leiris does not lie so much in the picturesque biographical detail as in what he can identify as fundamental in both his past and present, neither existing without the other. Both are aspects of the same continuous and continued reality. Thus, the reality of his own life still in progress is provisionally saved from oblivion by its older manifestations which are less exhumed than recovered alive in the present. It would be unjustifiable to assemble this material except from the double point of view of ethics and aesthetics. The reward he anticipated was to live and write better and thus, through an ennobling work, to make his life worthwhile.

Getting rid of the bonds of silence and keeping a part of his life from annihilation [*Fourbis*] Michel Leiris undertook then "to liquidate a certain number of things which oppressed him by writing about them." [*L'Age d'homme*] *Determined to find solid ground in the image he could draw of himself,* he wished especially "not to be in the position of a stranger in this world where he alternately slumbers and rushes about." In each of the memories recorded on numerous cards (most of which were only markers on a road leading to parts unknown) Michel Leiris expects "to find a useful meaning and at the same time a common dimension."

Biffures had been completed on a note of pessimism and what's-the-use which we find again at the end of *Fourbis.* A cyclothymic rhythm of relative euphoria and total despair which all artists experience to some extent: relatively reassured as long as they are constructing their work, uneasy as soon as the last wisps are dissipated, those last embellishing, exalting, anesthetizing wisps of creative intoxication, when they consider with what they believe to be objectivity (which is a new form of subjectivity) the little that they have done. Concerning *Biffures* (which was not much of a success), Michel Leiris writes in the beginning of *Fourbis* that "this book was nothing but an empty gesture compared with what he had hoped from it": to succeed, thanks to it, *in existing more profoundly*, through its medium to take *revenge on a life with which he was not satisfied*, for "it was less a question of defining himself in retrospect than of taking stock of himself in order to go beyond himself." In his happy periods of work (he would know others while writing *Fourbis*), Michel Leiris forgot his initial objective:

With this book . . . I re-embark, nonetheless, realizing that it is becoming more and more of an end in itself, and as little by little, it eclipses my other preoccupations, it becomes my reason for living when originally it was intended as a means of enlightening me as to a more coherent way of life—the mad race that I lead (dream gallop that gallops without budging) is it not a "race to the death?" Even if this book should in the end lead to a discovery, no doubt it would come so late that I should no longer have time to profit by it. And I do not even know for how many years I shall remain capable of drawing everything out of my memory like this as though by brute force!

Already in the last pages of *Biffures*, Michel Leiris had reached the point of doubt about the future of his prospecting. The method of investigation which he announces as far back as *L'Age d'homme* appears to be, however, of an inexhaustible fecundity. We find it hard to understand that he can fear "mental bankruptcy," from which, working indefinitely on the same stock of memories, he might be able to present nothing more than "a weaker and a more diluted rehash." In fact, it is not like a vein of ore that we follow to its end. The more we dig into our past, especially into our childhood, the more discoveries we make and continue to live and to live better, let us hope, thanks to the exploitation we make of these shrouded images.

What Michel Leiris wishes to clarify is that particular being, irreducible, obscure to himself, which he seeks in his most distant past and thoughts: for example in the substratum of language, a trap in which are caught from infancy the mysterious but instructive elements of our personal mythology, an irrationality where perhaps our reason for living is hidden. These are difficult to reach, a humble but fruitful way of coming to the remembrance of things past. Even in the balancing of certain of his sentences (more often, it is true, inspired by the master of his surrealist youth, André Breton), the influence of Proust is evident. Leiris, unconcerned about any possible ridicule, follows right through with his game of words. In the years around 1925 he published in *La Révolution surréaliste* a sort of dictionary with a significant title: *Glossaire, J'y serre mes gloses* (Glossary, I squeeze my glosses into it). After, for example, having defined *simulacre* (simulacrum, seeming semblance), he speaks of *cime âcre* (sharp summit), explaining:

By dissecting words we like, without worrying about following etymology, nor accepted connotations, we discover their most hidden virtues and the secret ramifications that are propagated throughout all language, channeled by the association of sounds, forms and ideas. Then language is transformed into an oracle and we have there a thread (tenuous though it may be) to guide us in the Babel of our mind.

It is a more explicit commentary than any of those that accompany the detailed research in associations that Michel Leiris propounds in *Biffures,* in which he refers to what certain words signified for him during his childhood and what they continue to evoke in his mind.

Leiris, like Joyce, is master of his means. His manias, and whatever is incontestably pathological in his behavior, far from reducing interest in his research, give it significance. Whoever meditates on the repetitive words of Michel Leiris must agree: there does not exist, there never did exist, there will not exist in the future, a more reasonable man. We are all madmen at large adjusting ourselves as best we can to our monsters by putting our best foot forward in order to fool people. We are all in terror and despair for days on end, our only moments of respite being those when we succeed in distracting ourselves from our obsessions, in particular, from the haunting fear of death. Hence that fever of activity to which most men abandon themselves, that more or less vain agitation by which they are duped in the end, especially when they attain the goal of the less illusory playthings, endowed with concrete material reality, money and power.

We find in this monograph, then, a being who is exceptionally vulnerable, unprotected, lost, who, while he judges himself with cruel lucidity, remains fascinated by his most ridiculous obsessions. This is a monograph about the Abnormal which could also no doubt be about the Normal, since nothing is more widespread than that crushed attitude toward life, that weakness, the panic of existing, the horror of knowing oneself to be mortal. Such confessions dealing with humble and everyday things may seem ridiculous to persons who tend to dissociate themselves from what they really are. Thus Michel Leiris's courage is all the greater.

Not that there is not some comedy in him. But he knows it and denounces it as such, his purpose being, since *L'Age d'homme, to reject his pretenses and reduce everything to its proper proportions.* In a page of his diary dated 1923, he berates himself for having at first wanted to play the role of Rolla, later that of Hamlet, then that of Gérard de Nerval:

I carry in my fingers the make-up with which I cover my life. . . . A fly which I crush in my hands proves my sadism. A glass of alcohol emptied in one gulp hoists me to the level of Dostoevski's great drunkards. And when I am tipsy, I shall make my general confession, omitting, of course, to say how, in order to ignore the banality of my life, I force myself to look at it only through glasses of the sublime. . . . I have always chosen masks that did not go with my ugly petit-bourgeois face, and I accepted in my heroes only what is easiest to imitate. [Quoted in *L'Age de raison*]

He tore off these masks, one after the other and in public, to appear in his truth, and, with perhaps unparalleled courage, laid bare his least admissible secrets: those that cost the most to recognize, although they are more or less shared by everyone. Remaining a man of letters even in his renunciation of literature, he resigns himself to a certain lack of affectivity, especially as he made it a rule for himself to renounce "grand airs, tremolos or sobs, as well as florid, gilded passages which would have no other result than to disguise the truth, even if only by attenuating its crudeness, by making it less shocking." Such is the purpose of the author of *De la littérature considerée comme une tauromachie.* Reduced to *the little that he does feel,* Michel Leiris does not always stop himself from orchestrating. Such is the case with the seemingly insignificant adventure to which he devotes the last beautiful chapter of *Fourbis.* He elevates it to the sublime only the better to cut it down later to a modest rank. Thus he goes from one extreme to another, constantly tinting this ambiguous passion "with the mad flame of love" only "to run it down again to the muddiest level."

What Michel Leiris can never express exaggeratedly enough is the vertigo of living. An existentialist anxiety, this manifests itself in his simplest gestures as well as his most insignificant thoughts. This is easy to recognize since, although it may take a different form, it is analogous to our own. Hence the parodoxical comfort of knowing that we are not as alone as we may think. Not only do we find a brother in Michel Leiris, but the similarity of our experience permits us to infer a more extensive fraternity, which really includes the entire human race. While still young, as the date of this old note from *Biffures* (1929) shows, Leiris declares himself disgusted by "the utter ignominy" of Sunday crowds:

All these people revolt me with their tranquillity and indifference, their complete unawareness. . . . I cannot understand how these people seem to have no idea that they are doomed to death, or seem at any rate to be resigned to it. This appears to me to be the height of brutishness and servility.

Always more and more obsessed with death, Michel Leiris soon renounced this facile scorn. Beyond the quasi-animal shadows that envelop him, we know that for a long time he has sought a fraternity not so much social as human. In spite of everything, he provides us with a certain comfort. In his political leanings (which border on communism) we see his desire to avoid easy solutions. Added to this is his longing for courage and action. Thus he passed from the revolt of his surrealistic period "to the concept of political revolution." [*L'Age d'homme*] Sometimes naïvely, but with beautiful lucidity, he attacks intellectual complacency and self-satisfaction. Thus he describes himself as "someone whose only impulses to action bear the form of a vague ideological militantism that induces him, from time to time, to take a position on the humanitarian problems of our epoch."

Michel Leiris reproaches himself for by-passing, more or less voluntarily, the great experiences of man: those of giving up life, risking death. Without suspecting that the one who gives up his life finally discovers a reason for risking it, he writes: "With a bitterness that I never suspected before I have just realized that all that I need in order to save myself is a certain fervor, but that this world lacks anything for which I would give my life." [*L'Age d'homme*] In *Fourbis:* "If there is nothing in love—or taste—for which I am ready to face death, I am only stirring up empty space and everything cancels itself out, myself included."

In this it seems to him lies the failure of his existence. Only a literary work, by describing his life, can turn it into a kind of success. Incapable of conquering his obsessions, he enumerates and labels them, following the advice of Jacques Rivière, who made it a rule *to consolidate his position with his reverses.*

His testimony has not been in vain: "If I should reach the point of contributing, no matter how little, to enable humanity, by throwing aside old teachings in favor of more fraternal behavior, to attain a kind of maturity, what difference should it make to others if my fate—considered simply as a work of art—is not a masterpiece?"

SAMUEL
BECKETT

AN IRISHMAN, A FRIEND AND DISCIPLE OF JOYCE, LIVING IN France, Beckett has for a long time been publishing, writing, expressing himself, perhaps thinking, only in French. He lives hidden in the suburbs of Paris, shunning publicity, haunted by the mysteries of life, extolling, as if in a dream and in a way so recondite as to seem almost inaudible, man who is *dream and silence.*

Material cares have been spared him since he created *Waiting for Godot,* a play first performed in Paris in 1953. Since then it has played all over the world with success proportionate to the stupefaction it provokes. He continues, nevertheless, to live as if he were poor. Such individuals are true to themselves.

This secretive man, this difficult writer, this celebrated personage whom no one knows except perhaps a few friends, and to whom crowds in all languages listen carefully without understanding a word of what his stage heroes have to say, this is Samuel Beckett.

Murphy, his first novel, which appeared and disappeared in England (1938), occasioned no greater notice in its French translation in 1947. All of Beckett is there already, however, in a more accessible form than what he was to choose subsequently. Since then he has renounced all compromise with the superficial and conventional. This author is at the opposite pole from writers who sugar-coat or prettify reality. In order to bring into relief its fundamental nature, he arbitrarily deprives life of what makes it livable. Take away the matter-of-fact or illusory charms which make it tolerable and there remains an unpolished existential base which at the same time challenges and yet implies the besetting and naked concept of death. The following works of Beckett, written directly in French, all are situated on the borders of oblivion. *Malone* takes place (presumably) just before, and *The Unnameable* (presumably) just after, death; *Molloy, Waiting for Godot, End Game, Tales and Texts for Nothing,* unfold (presumably) in some kind of limbo. I say "presumably," for with Beckett nothing is sure, Beckett himself is sure of nothing and his characters still less so. Reality is rendered colorless by fear, in which individuals, white with terror, propel themselves in reptilian motion before being immobilized forever.

With excessive outer consolations denied, there remains an inexpressible hope which in its purity greatly resembles the despair that it repudiates. Even if all asylum-keepers were eliminated, madness would still remain. Michel Leiris made us understand (like the Pirandello of *Henry IV*) that we are all madmen at large who, by putting them on the wrong scent, face our monsters more or less successfully.

This is voiced by one of the characters in *Waiting for Godot:* "We are all born mad. Some remain so." Michel Leiris makes us aware of these animalistic shadows which surround all men. The most lucid and courageous among us simply recognize but refuse to put up with them. By-passing whatever is not fundamental, we always come back to the same primary truths: either we speak in order to say nothing, or we all say the same thing. It is in this organic darkness that Samuel Beckett and his heroes move. The glimmerings of the mind are nothing but brief scintillations. With all the beautiful (too beautiful) constructions of reason laid low, there remain these pale fluorescences of a mind almost as opaque as the flesh. Fireflies flittering over a swampy surface.

Waiting for Godot was interpreted as an improbable play on words: does not *God* mean deity in English? A way of making this piece, which is as unreassuring as Beckett's other works, less disturbing. God would provide the solution. But we know nothing about Him. For whoever has not received the grace of faith, again, God is nothing but a word, useful for putting order into chaos and imparting meaning to the folly of existence, but, we must realize, it has never been made alluring because it is placed in the same class as dreams. What we can say not only to make more intelligible the significance of the daily waiting for this Godot who never comes, but also in an attempt to clarify the entire work of Beckett, is that there is in all his works a mysterious and imperious superior power which in some way reassures the very persons it terrifies.

Molloy feels, for example, that he cannot remain in the forest, where, like most of our author's heroes, he has been wandering interminably after either walking in circles for just as long round an equally enigmatic plain or skirting an anonymous ocean. "Sometimes it is the sea," we read in one of the *Texts for Nothing*, "sometimes the mountain, often it was the forest, the city, the plain also, I touched the plain also, I gave myself up for dead in all corners. . . ." Molloy, then, knows that it is no longer possible for him to remain in the forest:

That is to say I could have, physically nothing could have been easier, but I was not purely physical, I lacked something, and I would have had the feeling, if I had stayed in the forest, of going against an imperative, at least I had that impression. But perhaps I was mistaken, perhaps I would have been better advised to stay in the forest, perhaps I could have stayed there without remorse, without the painful impression of committing a fault, almost a sin. For I had greatly sinned, at all times, greatly sinned against my prompters. . . . But the imperatives are a little different, and I have always been inclined to submit to them, I don't know why.

In the same novel, *Molloy*, Moran is an agent, a member of a network in which he knows only the messenger who transmits orders to him. Orders come from a chief about whom he knows absolutely nothing. Malone, as he dies, is waited on by strangers "who probably are doing nothing but execute the orders of a consortium." They "decree" "in high places" with regard to him or his doubles. (This notion of *doubles* is of paramount importance in Beckett's mythology.) "Are you your own employer?" he asks one of the servants. [*Malone Dies*] In the same way the hero of *The Unnameable* obeys a master, perhaps even "a whole consortium of tyrants." Commands that are as obscure as they are imperious, analogous to those to which the heroes of *Waiting for Godot* submit, hoping for salvation from a superior who keeps away indefinitely from the rendezvous which he appoints them through an intermediary: "Yes, in this immense confusion, one thing alone is clear: we are waiting for Godot to come."

The human larva of *The Unnameable* reaches the point of believing that it must speak at any price (or rather write), even if it has nothing to express. We read at the beginning: "I am obliged to speak. I shall never be silent. Never." And at the end of the book, after two hundred and sixty pages:

I must continue, I can't continue, I must continue, so I am going to continue, I must say some words, as long as there are any, I must say them, until they find me, until they say to me, strange punishment, strange crime, I must continue, perhaps it is already done, perhaps they have already told me, perhaps they have brought me to the threshold of my story, before the door which opens on my story, it would surprise me if it opens, it is going to be me, it is going to be silence, there where I am, I don't know, I shall never know, in silence one doesn't know, I must continue, I am going to continue.

And better, or rather, still worse: "The fact seems to be, if one can speak of facts in the situation I am in, not only that I am going to speak about things of which I can't speak, but also, what is still more interesting, that I, . . . I don't know any longer, it doesn't matter. Meanwhile I am obliged to speak. I'll never be silent. Never."

Thus the author ends with a desperate and despairing repetition continued for close to three hundred pages. With *The Unnameable*, Beckett is at the point of being unable to say what is important to him except through apparently aimless monologues. "I appear to be speaking, it is not I, of me, it is not mine." The extreme subtlety of the analysis is combined with the most hackneyed language, the greatest precision with apparent license.

Therefore, speak, speak at any price, say no matter what,

since all words have equal value and all say the same thing, all repeat untiringly the same call for help. At times, Beckett drains the last drop out of a subject, chosen purposely among the most insignificant, the most uninteresting, the most indifferent of subjects: themes concerning the gray chicken or the pencil in *Malone Dies,* for example. "Yes, that's what I like about me, at least one of the things, that I can say, Up the Republic!, for example, or, Sweetheart!, for example, without having to wonder if I should not rather have cut my tongue out, or said something else. Yes, no reflection is needed, before or after, I have only to open my mouth for it to testify to the old story, my old story, and to the long silence that has silenced me, so that all is silent."

Even if Malone is silent, he writes. All of Beckett's characters write, following Beckett's own example. In that, too, they are created in his image. However inconvenient their physical position may be, Beckett, disregarding verisimilitude, puts a pencil in their fingers. Molloy must write. He receives an order to do so. And Moran must write. Malone "did not want to write but finally resigned himself to it." As for the hero of *The Unnameable,* he notes: "How, under these conditions, do I go about writing, considering only the manual aspect of this madness? I do not know. I could know but I shall not know. Not this time. It is I who write, I who cannot lift my hand from my knee. It is I who think, just enough to write, I whose head is far away." Even if Samuel Beckett objects to literature, he has a need to write. It is his justification and his *raison d'être,* nothing being certain unless it is written, what is most doubtful becoming clothed with a kind of consistency by virtue of its materialization into words. Man cannot exist in the world without the existence of the writer at his work table. Thus Beckett reveals himself a man of letters in spite of everything. In bearing witness for himself, he testifies in our behalf at the same time.

"What was I going to say? Never mind, I'll say something else, it's all the same." But that something else is more and more formless, useless, deprived of meaning. So much so that reading Beckett (fascinating in spite of the complexity of *Molloy*, his masterpiece) becomes heavier and heavier. Like Joyce, Beckett has reached a kind of outer limit, beyond which reading, and perhaps even writing itself, already arduous enough, is no longer conceivable. It is a question of letting language speak in order to see whether or not it is adequate for the expression of the reality that it claims to describe. A set purpose of admirable precision that ends by destroying not only the fictional value (it has passed beyond the novel) but the aesthetic and even the expressive values of these books. Samuel Beckett gladly gets along without the aesthetic value. But what about style?

In truth, it is not vocabulary that the author lacks to express the inexpressible, but rather the power of linking words in accordance with the absurdity of human reality. Whoever speaks is carried along by the logic of language and its articulations. Also the writer faced with the inexpressible must find some trick so as not to say what the words make him say in spite of himself, but rather to convey what words are designed to suppress: the uncertain, the contradictory, the unthinkable.

The unnameable.

The result is a sort of systematic deterioration of language which turns *The Unnameable* into a pointless discussion.

We fall here, as in so many modern works, into absolute silence, the very thing that we shall see Roland Barthes extolling in his *Degré zéro de l'écriture*. A silence it is well for us to be aware of, since it is in us as well as in Samuel Beckett. It is part of us, this silence which we have too much of a tendency to fill with songs, murmurings and noises, imported, superadded, illegitimate, *so as to hear it no longer*. By means of a literature that, by negating all literature, annihilates itself in the catastrophe it has created, Samuel Beckett, an exemplary *alittérateur*, opens a door in us which, even after Joyce and Kafka, might perhaps have remained closed. It is difficult to measure the part each has played in the systematic destruction of everything around us as well as in us, but which is not intrinsic to us. One cannot deny, at any rate, the extraordinary impression, I dare not say of enrichment, since it concerns awareness of an absolute poverty, that Samuel Beckett creates. Poverty that is our only wealth. Inexhaustible, fascinating poverty.

An open door is not a picture. After a brief but vivid glance through it, I am on the threshold, facing the light about which Beckett himself often speaks, pointing out that it is darkness compared to daylight but brightness alongside of night. We had known for a long time (at least since Freud, who made explicit what had been implicitly expressed for centuries), of this coexistence of night and day within us. The mind of Murphy, then, with its three zones, is not completely strange to us.

It was made up of light fading into dark, of above and beneath, but not of good or bad. It contained forms with parallels in another mode and forms without, but not right forms and wrong forms. It felt no issue between its light and dark, no need for its light to devour its dark. The need was now to be in the light, now in the half light, now in the dark. That was all. . . . He was split, one part of him never left this mental chamber that pictured itself as a sphere full of light fading into dark, because there was no way out.

The novelty is not the awareness of inner shadows, but in accepting them. Yet, even from the time of *Murphy*, Beckett does not lose interest in the outer world: the hero of this first novel is still of the world, he has social relations, he moves about elsewhere than within himself. But what Murphy called *his private universe* finally took priority over the other, which is no more real just because it is made up of material things. Following Samuel Beckett, the reader plunges into this obscurity as well as he can. His guide shows him nothing that he does not already know. He only forces him not to glance aside, to remain a little longer in this airless universe, where, holding his breath, he looks for a long moment into the caverns of being, without, however, having the time to explore them. Before having read Kafka, Joyce, and Beckett with patience and continuity, we did have, I dare say, a few rays in this darkness. But we were careful not to plunge headlong, being satisfied to send out a few feelers from a prudent distance into the depths of the ocean. Certain writers did, however, dive in without being invited by Kafka or Joyce, to return no more, such as the accursed poets recently recognized in France—Antonin Artaud and Roger Gilbert-Lecomte.

It seems that with Samuel Beckett, whether we like it or not, even more than with Kafka or Joyce, we must exert ourselves. His heroes, interchangeable from book to book, are all projections of the author, who, in turn, is a reflection of ourselves. André Rousseaux was right in saying that it is not at all by chance that they all have names that resemble one another. The man in whom Beckett is interested is not individualized, he has no identity. Beckett is dealing with absolute Man, confronted with the double mystery of birth and death, passing almost directly from one to the other, having just enough time in the interval to proffer a few words that scarcely make any more or less sense than first wails and last death rattles. Time exists no more than does space in Beckett's universe. His characters know neither where nor when they are, nor even if they are. Each affirmation to which they dare agree is immediately followed by an annihilating negation. It suffices here to open any one of his works at random. For example, *Tales and Texts for Nothing:*

How long have I been here? What a question, it's one I've often asked myself. And often I was able to answer. An hour, a month, a year, a hundred years, according to what I understood by here, by me, by being. Everything is mixed up, times are mixed up, at first I had only been there, now I am still there, in a little while I shall not still be there, struggling halfway up, or in the ferns that border the woods, they are pine trees, I don't try to understand, I shall no longer ever try to understand, that is what they say, for the moment, I am there, always have been, always shall be, I'll no longer be afraid of big words, they aren't big. I don't remember having come, I shall never be able to leave. . . .

Or *Malone Dies:*

But what matter whether I was born or not, have lived or not, am dead or merely dying, I shall go on doing as I have always done, not knowing what it is I do, nor who I am, nor where I come from, nor if I am.

Pozzo, one of the heroes of *Waiting for Godot,* cries out: "Have you not done tormenting me with your accursed time? It's abominable! When! When! One day, is that not enough for you, one day he went dumb, one day I went blind, one day we'll go deaf, one day we were born, one day we shall die, the same day, the same second, is that not enough for you?"

Yesterday and tomorrow, here and somewhere else, are all the same for these sick people, these wounded, amputated people, whose physical deformities make possible a philosophy that eludes them. Progressive annihilation, so much so that in the end there is no more than a single mouth that complains. Not even that: a voice. A formless, impalpable, nonexistent being, but a being that suffers.

To live, for Malone, is "to wander about, the only one alive, in the depths of a limitless moment, in which the light does not vary, in which the wrecks all look alike." Everything is brought into play, not only from the reality on the outside, but from the universe on the inside. Beckett makes his characters always descend deeper and deeper into their innermost depths, speleologists of themselves. Descent into the Hades of the individual which never ends, for the explorer keeps on finding other subterranean zones indefinitely. His quest is for the fundamental reality which would remain, once what is accessory in man has been destroyed. By dropping down into the elementary void of existence, perhaps it is the soul that he hopes to find in the end. But he has never found it, experiencing only an inexpressible nostalgia.

In Beckett's works there are innumerable questions similar to these from *Tales and Texts for Nothing:* "Where should I go if I could go, what should I be if I could be, what should I say if I had a voice, who speaks thus, calling himself me?" Molloy, in the pangs of self-analysis, also murmurs: "My life, my life, now I speak of it as of something over, now as of a joke which still goes on, and it is neither, for at the same time it is over and it goes on, and is there any tense for that?"

So, "no matter what vestiges of flesh and conscience go into it, there is no point in stalking people. If he is still what is called alive, make no mistake about it, he is guilty." Many characters reappear again and again in the chiaroscuros and white shadows of Beckett's novels. They all lead to the same man. The first lines of *The Unnameable* are significant: "Where now? When now? Who now? Without asking myself. Saying I." Reading the novels we may wonder if we are not dealing with a few chapters of one and the same serial. All of Samuel Beckett's novels tell the same story. They are really all one continuous novel, a novel that began with Murphy, who conceived of his mind *as a large hollow sphere, hermetically closed to the universe without:* "Nothing ever had been, was or would be in the universe outside it that was not already present as virtual, or actual, or virtual rising into actual, or actual falling into virtual, in the universe inside it."

"His mind being closed, a closed system subject to no principle of change but its own, self-sufficient and impermeable to the vicissitudes of the body," the excluded exterior world recomposes itself into phantasms. As far back as *Murphy* we learn that "all movement in the world of the mind depends on rest in the world of the body." Hence the absolute deterioration of most of Beckett's heroes; hence their forced immobility, caused by multiple infirmities which they bear rather well, since they are beyond suffering. They all have in common what Beckett tells us about Murphy: "As he lapsed in body he felt himself coming alive in mind, set free to move among its treasures. The body has its stock, the mind its treasures." What difference does it make then what he will say or how! "Everything is a pretext." [*Malone Dies*] "God and men, daylight and nature, the leaps of the heart and the means of understanding, like a coward I have invented them, without anybody's help, since there is nobody to postpone the hour of speaking about myself. . . . Love I invented, music, the odor of wild currants, in order to spare myself." [*The Unnameable*] Of what importance are his characters themselves:

These Murphys, Molloys and other Malones, I am not fooled by them. They made me lose my time, waste my efforts, by allowing myself to speak about them, when I should have spoken only of myself, in order to be able to stop talking. But I have just said that I spoke about myself, that I am in the midst of speaking about myself. The hell with what I have just said. Now I am going to speak about myself for the first time. I thought I was doing well, associating myself with those pain-sufferers. I was wrong. They did not suffer my pains, their pains are nothing compared with mine, nothing but a small part which I thought I could detach from myself in order to contemplate it. Now let them go away, they and the others, those who served me, those who are waiting, let them return to me what I inflicted on them and disappear, from my life, from my memory, from my shames, from my fears. There you are, there is no longer anyone but me here, no one revolves around me, no one comes toward me, no one has ever met anyone in my presence. These people never were. Never were anything except me and this opaque empty space.

What is left once the Murphys, Molloys and other Malones are dismissed? Only he, Samuel Beckett, of course, but only in so far as Malone, Molloy, Murphy, were already he. By the same right as they, a new fictional being, that is, a new character in this uninterrupted novel of the night, a character, moreover, who splits into several characters (the *doubles*). "Yes, no matter what I say, I shall try to make a little creature, to hold in my arms, a little creature made in my image." [*Malone Dies*]

I have made notes on each of Samuel Beckett's works that I have read. I notice, however, that not a single note among them refers to what essential meaning the discovery of this author had for me. I felt it (I don't say I understood it) in several places, but in such a fleeting way, so tenuously, that I was not able to discern the words in the text that would have enabled me to retain it. I can illustrate what Beckett's thinking is by means of numerous concordant quotations and I can establish the details of his personal mythology. I could, for example, write three pages on the unusual role of hats in his work, or on what he considers so important about *possessions,* the possessions of his heroes having value only by virtue of their insignificance, which measures and exalts their loss. But I find it impossible to quote a single passage from his novels which, without clarification, would even suggest its essential meaning.

What is it all about? I must try to recall how I crossed the threshold of Samuel Beckett's world and see what I felt. It was not so much an absolute expatriation as the absolute rediscovery of our own country: our true domain, that from which we have been distracted, from earliest childhood, by a system of thinking imposed upon us by language and its good usage. In order that we may live, we must no longer know anything about life. A frightful domain. A total void. This absolute misery—body and soul—of Beckett's characters, almost all reduced to crawling if not to immobility, these curtailments are but a material representation of our state of utter nudity as soon as we face the full force of our existence, which at the same time denies death and presupposes it. A well-known anxiety. What is new is that he makes us intensely sensitive to it, giving it, thanks to images, an actuality that is not only closely wedded to reassuring social structures but at the same time annihilates them.

So far, I have said nothing. Of course, these things are indescribable. After so many pages, even Samuel Beckett himself must have the impression of scarcely having begun to express what obsesses him. He should know, however, that he has materialized the impalpable, that he has almost enabled us to touch the walls of our prisons. From that point on the question of the literary and aesthetic value of his books no longer arises. Perhaps Beckett will be followed by authors, akin to him, who will go beyond him, just as, in many ways, he goes beyond Kafka and Joyce. It makes little difference. For his time, which is our time, his work is of prime importance. We can say about writers who succeed each other what we have said about Beckett's heroes: that they are all one and the same individual. We have a perfect right to choose our friends or accomplices among the great writers, to prefer Baudelaire to Rimbaud or Proust to Joyce. These are personal tastes, affinities, matters of the heart. The only thing that counts is that ephemeral but revealing walk into the darkness, once the threshold is crossed. We identify ourselves with the mad aspiration that Molloy has to get to the bottom of things. Like Murphy it is enough for us to know of life that it is *a long groping repetition;* like Malone, we *have been groping our way all our lives.* Groping, groping . . . Among what Beckett's heroes call *their possessions,* there is one article that is more important to them than their hat: their stick. The blind man's stick. These two sentences from *Ulysses* might be used as a motto for this difficult work: "You find my words obscure? The obscurity is in our souls, don't you think?"

With each of his new works Samuel Beckett seems to reach an ultimate frontier which the next book, however, succeeds in pushing back. With *Malone Dies*, it seemed impossible to go further in the novel. However, along came *The Unnameable*, so aptly christened, whose formless, stammering hero would have nothing human about him if he did not retain that sorrowful and acute awareness of his condition. With *Waiting for Godot* we thought we had reached the limit beyond which no play was conceivable. But now comes *End Game* which surpasses it by far in austerity.

Out of this incandescent melting pot come situations and dialogues whose essence is barely perceptible. The amazing thing—and here lies Beckett's genius—is that these characters are not so unlifelike that we cannot get excited about the motionless adventures of their vegetative existence. Whatever little flesh they have covers what may be called their soul.

GEORGES BATAILLE

GEORGES BATAILLE CONSTANTLY REFERS TO GOD, OR RATHER TO his *eternal absence and the void that he denotes.* By *inner experience* he means what is habitually called *mystical experience:* meditation, ecstasy, rapture. From the beginning of the first volume of his *Somme athéologique* (Summa Atheologica), the only volume that has appeared to date, published in 1943 under the title *L'Expérience intérieure* (The Inner Experience), the author states that he is thinking less about the confessional experience "than about a bare experience, in no way connected with any confession whatsoever." That is why, he adds, he does not like the word *mystic.* The states of mind described by mystics "independent, it is true, of the assumptions with which mystics suppose them to be bound up," have none the less not ceased to be closed to him. Bataille points out in *Méthode de méditation* that for him this spiritual experience is at the antipodes of his conception of salvation and pure mysticism. At the beginning of a passage on *fundamental eroticism,* he once more assures us that the God to whom he refers is not of any particular religion. He almost goes so far as to say: *especially* not of the Christian religion. If Georges Bataille does not use this adverb, he implies it. In *L'Erotisme ou la mise en question de l'être* (Eroticism or the Question of Being) he repeats that the religion he is discussing is not *a* religion but *all* religion:

I am not speaking here of rites, dogmas, or a given community, but solely of the problem which every religion faces: I make this problem my business, as the theologian does with theology. . . . But without the Christian religion. If it were not a religion in spite of everything, I should even feel myself to be at the antipodes of Christianity. This is so much so that the study in which I define this position is concerned with *eroticism.* It goes without saying that the development of eroticism is *in no way* outside the domain of religion but simply that, by being opposed to eroticism, Christianity has condemned most religions. In a sense, the Christian religion is perhaps the least religious.

Let us pass over the "it goes without saying" typical of André Breton's disciples and here and there motivated only by the whim of the writer. We find again that arbitrary distrust of any Christian solution to the question of religion that has been mentioned in connection with Antonin Artaud. On the one hand, the taste for blasphemy inherited from a whole generation and taken up piously by surrealists and their following; on the other hand, an irrepressible mystical nostalgia evident in surrealism itself and especially in its founder, André Breton. The rejection of Christianity is too vehement among these fanatics not to be suspect. People who are not preoccupied with the supernatural and do not believe in it at all have no need to become upset about religion, whatever it may be. The result is the coexistence, among these fanatics, of a vociferous execration of Christianity and a favorable attitude toward the most elementary forms of the will to believe. A contradiction that does not disturb them, as though they envied not simply the idols and sacrifices of primitive peoples but also what one could call their prelogical mentality.

The metaphysics that obsess Georges Bataille seem, as is so often the case, to be of physical origin. Thus, aspirations toward the infinite are born in the finite of the individual's personality. He knows it, and, a rational madman, he strives to systematize his mania. When he was young, he had faith and in *L'Expérience intérieure* he alludes to the disorder of his life "upon leaving a long-lasting Christian piety." The anti-Christian prejudice which subsisted in him, has therefore, as in Artaud and so many others, its origin in the opposite spiritual attitude. "I do not hate God, basically I do not know him," he notes in *Sur Nietzsche*. But he did not ignore Christ, whom he was perhaps not far from hating. Georges Bataille's Hegelian logic does not help him to escape the contradictions common to a great number of intellectuals of his period.

The problem of subterfuge is among those that preoccupy him. In reference to one of his memories he says that it has the same moldy smell of comedy as his whole life. [*L'Expérience intérieure*] He adds in *Le Coupable* (The Guilty) that it is debasing to reduce the lacerating voluptuousness of chagrin *to the vulgarity of a literary theme:* "When voluptuousness is lived through the eyes of the ascetic, when torture gnaws naïvely, what is at stake is in the sky, in the dark, in the cold, and not in the history of letters." Wishing, like Michel Leiris (to whom he pays special tribute at the head of his work *L'Erotisme*), to name one of his works *l'heure de la vérité* (the moment of truth) in which he refers to the moment in a bullfight when the bull is about to die, Georges Bataille is obliged to admit that he is hiding something: "Cheating? With death how can one avoid cheating? Cheating! I decided the other day to die; what anguish brought, the wind carried away." [*Le Coupable*] Or, in the opposite sense: "My levity and my amused victory over anxiety were false." [*Sur Nietszche*] In *La Haine de la poésie* (Hatred of Poetry) he equates his need of writing with that of lying: "I must say also: these words that I align lie. . . . On the eve, I seemed to be aware of my game: it was a farce, nothing but a lie." . . . And again:

Until then I had never had this clearcut awareness of my own comedy: my life presented precisely as a spectacle and my own curiosity that has enabled me to reach the point where I am, where the comedy is so full and so true that it says:
"I am the comedy."

One of Georges Bataille's subterfuges consists of partially depriving us of the clues that he possesses, since he does not practice literary trickery against himself. Allusive notes are permissible in an intimate notebook. When these are published, arbitrary silence on what would clarify them seems more difficult to explain. By reviewing the different ways in which Georges Bataille passes over essentials, we end up with some glimmering of light as to what he was silent about. In general, we are dealing with some very poorly kept secrets. All suffering is at once banal and irreducible. Here it is the frustration of a desire that is always renascent and always disappointed, that of love-sickness. Waiting, pleasure, jealousy, solitude, are these legitimate reasons for such profound anxiety? In Georges Bataille, as in so many others, his almost physical pain is transformed into something metaphysical.

While Georges Bataille was not trying to hide the humble origin of his torment, he is often enigmatic. Rather often he complicates our effort toward elucidation by suspension points. A concern for decency may sometimes explain his cuts. For example, in *Sur Nietzsche:* "I turned in the direction of . . . in the hope . . . (No interest in being naked: I put my clothes on again.)" Maybe. Needs must. But on the next page: "Ten days ago, on the contrary, I was surprised upon my return to Paris . . . I have selfishly come to desire stability." Or in "Histoire de rats" (Story of Rats): "Lucidity excludes desire (or perhaps kills it, I don't know): what remains, A. dominates, while I . . ." A debatable procedure, and one that gives an impression of profundity at little cost, even when it is the inexpressible that is suggested by these silences where punctuation no longer indicates a cut in the text but an interruption in the thought. See those whole paragraphs of suspension points at the end of *Méthode de méditation,* for example, or in "Histoire de rats."

We have, moreover, the impression that except for cases of *force majeure* (the inexpressible) we are dealing with an arbitrary plan on the part of Georges Bataille, a method of intimidating or confronting the reader. Sometimes the dots pinpointing the silence of the indescribable are changed by Georges Bataille from one edition to the next. For example, in the original edition of *Méthode de méditation* we find:

. . . This one, the present one, neither heaven nor I, nor death nor light—and heaven and I, death and light, etc.

In the new edition he makes this correction:

. . . This one, the present one, neither my absence nor I, nor death nor light—and my absence and I, death and light, etc.

The more we think it over the better we understand how Georges Bataille can pass from heaven to his own absence and make synonyms out of these two words that are so different. In this way poetry proceeds by the rapprochement of unrelated images, the most surprising being at times the most striking. We must, therefore, be careful not to reproach our author for writing *literature* here in the disparaging sense of the word. Besides, Georges Bataille does not worry so much about his reader as about himself. It is with himself that he is dealing. He makes out as best he can, and if he invites us to watch him, he does not invite us to participate in the confrontation. In more than one passage he tells us about the hatred he experiences towards his own slowness and obscurity, notably in the "Post-Scriptum" (1953) of *Méthode de méditation* (1947). He is not trying to fool us but to allay his anxiety (as one cheats one's hunger).

Neither laughable nor tragic, but both at the same time for infinity. ["Post-Scriptum"] Of his joy, "one will not be able to tell whether he is dying or laughing on account of it." [*Sur Nietzsche*] *Games* occupy a large place in his manner of being and appearing: "But *playing* is first of all *not taking oneself seriously.* And *dying.*" Georges Bataille uses this method advisedly, since he writes in the course of the aforementioned postscript: "In the manner of thought that I introduce, what counts is never the affirmation. What I say, I believe no doubt, but I know that I bear within me the impulse that wants the affirmation to disappear farther on." We read in this connection, in *L'Abbé C.* (a curiously unsuccessful novel that no doubt had the same erotic sources of inspiration as "Histoire de rats" and "Dianus") :

The only way to compensate for the mistake of writing is to destroy what is written. But that can only be done by the author: a destruction that leaves the essential intact, I can, nevertheless, bind the negation so tightly to the affirmation that my pen erases as fast as it goes ahead. It operates then, in a word, the way "time" generally operates—which, of its multiple edifices, allows only traces of death to subsist. I believe that the secret of literature lies there and that a book is only beautiful when it is adorned cleverly with the indifference of ruins.

In Georges Bataille's estimation, if he were allotted a place in the history of thought, it would be for "discerning in our human life the effects of the disappearance of discursive reality," and for having drawn from the description of these effects a *disappearing light:* "This light dazzles perhaps but it announces the opacity of *night:* it announces only night." ["Post-Scriptum"] In this night his thought always ends by getting lost, but he observes its slow or sudden disappearance, he points it out, he comments on it. It is impossible for us to know whether these are the shadows of a faltering mind or the limits beyond which no intelligence can go. One of the principles of *Méthode de méditation* is thus explained by its author: "The apparent relaxation of standards can express only a higher standard to which we should have responded in the first place. This principle should also be reversed. The apparent perfectionism that he affirms is only the effect of a deep relaxation, of the abandonment of something essential, the *sovereignty of the individual.*" In the dialectic of Georges Bataille synthesis does not propose what thesis and antithesis lead one to expect. He calmly affirms: "Liberty is nothing if it does not

border on the limits where all comprehension falls apart."
[*La Haine de la poésie*]

Georges Bataille likes to say that he is not understood. "Infinite misunderstanding: whatever I like, wherever like the lark I cry out my joy, I must do so in depressing terms." [*Sur Nietzsche*] But how can we see clearly where he gropes as he walks? The author of *Méthode de méditation* sometimes assumes the responsibility for these misunderstandings *which spring from the disorder of his books* and he tries to clear them up. In general these attempts at enlightenment result in making him more obscure. In fact, he never stops playing with words. If the acrobatics continue, it becomes a work without continuity and we have no desire to laugh at it. If we do laugh, it is with meaningless and feeble laughter. Bataille writes in *Sur Nietzsche:* "But I laugh. As the word returns endlessly under my pen, they say that I laugh out of the wrong side of my mouth. I am amused and saddened at the same time by the misunderstanding. My laughter is gay."

Of Nietzsche, his master, to whom he refers in all his books, Georges Bataille wrote that this proposition pleased him above all: "And may we hold as false every truth that is not welcomed with a burst of laughter." [*Zarathustra*] If he speaks with scorn about Bergson ("little prudent man") he realizes that reading his work on *Laughter,* as irritating and curt as it appeared to him, did have this effect: "Laughter's hidden meaning was from that time on the key question for me." [*L'Expérience intérieure*]

Since then, Georges Bataille has placed laughter among what he calls the *sovereign* effusions, conducts or operations.

He adds to it: intoxication, poetry, sacrifice (rites, performances, tales, and even films, without mentioning, still in connection with sacrifice, an undeniable sado-masochistic obsession, but he speaks little about them) and finally, eroticism, the central element of his personal mysticism.

It is not happiness that Georges Bataille or his heroes want to attain, it is the *impossible*, from which they do not wish to be diverted at any price. "I wrote *Supplice* (Torture) in which man attains the extreme of the possible," we read in the first pages of *L'Expérience intérieure*. And at the beginning of *Méthode de méditation:* "My ambition in the following pages is the most far-reaching ever conceived." So it is a question of *going the farthest possible*, of *going as far as one can go*. All the formulas are taken from *L'Expérience intérieure*, where we also find:

The extreme of the possible.—At last we are there. But so late? . . . What, without knowing it, one arrives there?—(in truth, nothing has changed)—by a detour: one laughs (very loud), another gets into a jam and beats his wife, or gets dead drunk, or perishes in torture.

What is to be done in the prison of the body, he notes in *Sur Nietzsche*, unless it is to evoke the expanse which begins on the other side of the walls? "If God does not exist, this lacerated lamentation in solitude is the extreme limit of the possible." Georges Bataille shows an *infinite interest*, not only in what exceeds the limited being, but in the *very excesses by which we want to pass beyond its limits*. Hence his fascination with eroticism, the hopeless invincible taste for the orgy, as exemplified in his so-called licentious books, *Histoire de l'œil* (Story of the Eye), *Madame Edwarda*, and *Le Bleu du Ciel* (Sky Blue). In *Sur Nietzsche* he sets this rule:

The only strict and honest way. Have *no* finite exigency. Do not admit a limit in any sense or direction. Not even in the direction of the infinite. Demand of the individual what he is or what he will be. *Know nothing,* unless it be fascination. Never stop at the apparent limits.

Georges Bataille demands the impossible of the woman whom he loves. "What unites me to B. is the impossible as a void in front of her and me, instead of an assured life in common." ["Histoire de rats"] Our author, who wants to be sure not to confuse his debauchery with his mystical life [*Le Coupable*] has the courage to let himself be seen at times in his lowest moments, defying all convention, like one of his heroes, "sunk, drunk, and ruddy in a dive of naked women." ["Histoire de rats"] But from eroticism he passes on to love, from desire to passion. His obsession almost always ends by concentrating on a particular woman. In the intimate diary of *Sur Nietzsche,* as well as in the transpositions of *La Haine de la poésie,* he describes pure love in the classic sense of the term. Thus he escapes from the sordid to arrive at the sublime. Moreover, we must not forget, eroticism is one way among others chosen by Georges Bataille to force the doors of the impossible.

This nostalgia for the inaccessible is the equivalent of *a desire for sovereign knowledge.* Unintelligence, of others and his own, is one of Georges Bataille's obsessions. "The being who is there, in his immense folly, man is the *impossible* incarnate in every sense. He is the inadmissible. . . ." But at the other pole of this "labyrinth of aberrations, deafnesses, horrors," at the peak of intelligence, here again is "a region of supreme foolishness, of sleep." Ecstasy itself then becomes "the gay but anxious feeling of his immeasurable stupidity."

If this mind, which would like to be totally unfettered and powerful, denotes its limits in *Méthode de méditation*, it does not feel intellectually inferior to other men, even the greatest, but quite the contrary. We have heard Bataille declare that with such a book he reached the extreme possible to the human mind. He hopes to have a place in the history of thought. He would undoubtedly concur with the proud declaration of Paul Valéry: "The spur in every intellectual life is the conviction of the failure, or the abortion, or the insufficiency of previous intellectual lives." Bataille suffers from no inferiority complex: "Science is made by men in whom the desire to know is dead." Even if he recognizes the greatness of Nietzsche, he treats him almost as an equal. When someone exposes the parallelism of certain of his conceptions with those of Heidegger, he answers that Heidegger's work is professorial, while his method remains *glued* to results:

What counts in my eyes on the contrary is the moment of *ungluing*, what I teach (if it is true that . . .) is an intoxication, it is not a philosophy: I am not a philosopher but a *saint*, perhaps a madman.

We are all crazy: the wisest thing we can do is keep quiet. Georges Bataille for a moment renounces the idea of controlling himself; he abandons himself for an instant, allows an avowal of his particular madness to escape, thinking that it is of no consequence since he immediately recovers control. If he says what reason would counsel him not to say (I am a *saint*, perhaps a madman, underlining the word saint no doubt in order to show which he preferred), was it not done in complete lucidity? It is true that the context is important: that of the work, that of the life. From the pen of Antonin Artaud, who could have written them, these last lines of Georges Bataille would seem to confirm paranoia. "I am leaving in search of the impossible," Artaud wrote upon embarking for Mexico. These words could be by Georges Bataille. And whose cry is this: "I only like to live provided that I am burning"? Artaud's? No, Bataille's. [*La Haine de la poésie*] Again we find the common domain of aliterature, into which we are progressively initiated by the authors studied in this volume. By now we know their common refrain: the complaint of man's solitude since God has died.

ALBERT
CAMUS

IN AN ESSAY DEVOTED TO THE YOUTH OF MAURICE BARRÈS,
Professor Henri Mondor recalls that Albert Camus is one of
the rare present-day writers who acknowledge their debt of
gratitude to the author of *Le Jardin de Bérénice*. In Camus'
earlier works and in *La Chute* (The Fall), we find that
sumptuosity of words and simplicity of style that is reminis-
cent of the one to whom Marcel Proust said: "In what you
write there are certain tone changes that exist only in
music." Barrès' style is described by Henri Mondor as follows: fine vocabulary, magic of syllables, powerful images,
richness in syntax and tone, disturbing utilization of mystery, extreme sweetness of melody, picturesque familiarities,
brusque strength in turnabouts, and justifiable short cuts
and insolence. All this seems in Camus as in Barrès a little
too "literary," in the derogatory sense of the term, but in
spite of this it attains a rare quality in *La Chute*. The earlier

works are mere pieces of bravado whose very perfection and intended anthological character call a little too much for admiration, exercises of a virtuoso who is delighted with his own gifts. The strictness of standards is not relaxed but for fleeting and venial verbal indulgences. "With the true confessions," Maurice Barrès admitted, "were mixed in my work too many pages of which I may say: 'When I think about all of that, I despise myself.'" These last words are also pure Camus. A new Camus, capable of cruel humor toward himself and ceasing to take himself seriously: the Camus of *The Fall*.

The author of *Le Mythe de Sisyphe* indicated in certain pages of *L'Eté*, in particular throughout the chapter called "L'Enigme," his disappointment at seeing himself confined by his admirers, or those who claimed to be, within his philosophy of the absurd: "What else did I do, after all, but elaborate on an idea that I found in the streets of my time? That I nurtured this idea (and that a part of me still nurtures it) along with my whole generation, goes without saying. I simply took the perspective needed to discuss it and determine its logic. Everything that I was able to write afterwards demonstrates it amply. But it is proper to exploit a formula rather than a nuance. The formula was chosen: here I am as absurd as before." This reaction of displeasure, if not exasperation, gives way in *La Chute* to a feeling which is at once more measured and profound, almost mournful. Certainly, we still find in the first pages the superior airs of the earlier Camus: "Anyone who has considerably meditated on man, by profession or vocation, is led to feel nostalgia for the primates. They at least don't have any ulterior motives." Reading what follows we discover that he is not talking about what some more or less sympathetic but indifferent readers think or say about him. These embarrassing ulterior motives he discovers in his own friends: *"A man like you* . . . people would say sweetly, and I would blanch. I didn't want their esteem because it wasn't general. . . ."* I interrupt the quotation here for a moment. We must emphasize the Camus whom his friends surprise, disappoint and pain, those friends whom, like each of us, he needs so much at certain times when they are not there:

Don't think for a minute that your friends will telephone you every evening, as they ought to, in order to find out if this doesn't happen to be the evening when you are deciding to commit suicide, or simply whether you don't need company, whether you are not in a mood to go out. No, don't worry, they'll ring you up the evening you are not alone, when life is beautiful. As for suicide, they would be more likely to push you to it, by virtue of what you owe to yourself, according to them. May heaven protect us, *cher monsieur,* from being set on a pedestal by our friends!

And farther on: "I realized that I had no friends. Besides, even if I had had, I shouldn't be any better off. If I had been able to commit suicide and then see their reaction, why, then the game would have been worth the candle." We can now complete the aforementioned sentence which carries us farther forward in our acquaintance with the new Camus: "I didn't want their esteem because it wasn't general, and how could *it be general since I couldn't share it?"* Weren't we paying attention before? The fact is that this Camus who doubts his own excellence surprises us. Doubtless, the self-assurance for which we have reproached him is more apparent than real. Undoubtedly, this is his personal way of building himself up in order to avoid this disheartening prospect of oblivion. It looks as if the critics, notably Sartre, who attacked him harshly, had, by their severity, incited Albert Camus to search himself seriously. Whatever may have been the lack of good will toward him on the part of his adversaries, their hostility is worth taking into consideration. If this was the way they saw him, wasn't it because such was his appearance? Perhaps that is what Camus told himself. A reaction was apparent in not only the aesthetic but also the ethical consequences of *La Chute*. Regardless of this, the often reticent, sometimes hostile, almost venomous reception which he was accorded in France upon the occasion of his receiving the Nobel Prize, showed that his adversaries were not disarmed.

We have commented on *La Chute* up to this point as if we were dealing with an essay by the author about himself, which it is not. Yet we are dealing with a story whose apparently objective design never hides its subjectivity. In the end Camus drops the mask: in all likelihood, it was Camus himself that the narrator was addressing, but this does not necessarily signify that Jean-Baptiste Clamence was Albert Camus himself. Let us say rather that he appears as his mouthpiece, the one whom he entrusted not only with replying to his enemies (and to his friends, who were hardly different) but also, in so far as there was some truth in their attitude toward him, to play their game and bear the brunt of their reproaches. Thanks to this subterfuge, not only identified by him but there by choice, Albert Camus can poke fun at himself nicely and efficaciously. His humor becomes, for the duration of a book, his particular way of *consolidating his position with his reverses*.

A voluntary exile in Amsterdam (where the beauties of

sky and water enable him to compose some lovely variations), the narrator is a former lawyer: "I had a specialty: noble cases. . . . Yet it was enough for me to sniff the slightest scent of the victim on a defendant for me to swing into action. . . . You would really have thought that justice slept with me every night. . . . Nature favored me as to my physique, and the noble attitude comes effortlessly. Furthermore, I was buoyed up by two sincere feelings: the satisfaction of being on the right side of the bar and an instinctive scorn for judges in general." This portrait is a good likeness. Nor does it miss, a little farther on, the allusion to the "two or three manifestos, perhaps even more," launched and signed at the least excuse. Nor indeed, frank irony: "Let us pause on these heights. Now you understand what I meant when I spoke of aiming higher. I was talking, it so happens, of those supreme summits, the only places I can really live. Yes, I have never felt comfortable except in lofty places." He goes so far as to make fun, in passing, of his own style:

When I used to live in France, were I to meet an intelligent man I immediately sought his company. If that be foolish . . . Ah, I see you smile at that use of the subjunctive. I confess my weakness for that mood and for fine speech in general. A weakness that I criticize in myself, believe me. I am well aware that an addiction to silk underwear does not necessarily imply that one's feet are dirty. Nonetheless, style, like sheer silk, too often hides eczema. My consolation is to tell myself that, after all, those who murder the language are not pure either.

Purity, self-esteem. A nostalgia which has always been part of Camus' greatness, in spite of the weaknesses which he dares admit today for the first time: which confirms and, no doubt, even increases his nobility instead of threatening it. This man who often set himself up as a judge suffers in turn by being judged, but draws a lesson from this state of things: "In short, the moment I grasped that there was something to judge in me, I realized that there was in them [those like him] an irresistible vocation for judgment." Jean-Baptiste Clamence takes *his beautiful soul* apart and is not proud of what he discovers: "Then I realized, as a result of delving in my memory, that modesty helped me shine, humility to conquer, and virtue to oppress." Let us not confuse the narrator and the author here. Camus has his faults but they are not exactly those of his hero. We heard him admit a moment ago the one which, among others, we had long ago discovered not only in him but quite generally among those intellectuals who claim a clear conscience a little too easily: *the satisfaction of being on the right side of the bar.* From this follows a facile scorn for certain adversaries. But this attitude, improper or not, implies, in the first place, a feeling of spiritual uneasiness. Albert Camus, who had constructed his entire work so as to escape his own contradictions without deceit, found in his fifteenth work his initial dissatisfaction:

God is not needed to create guilt or to punish. Our fellow men suffice, aided by ourselves. You were speaking of the Last Judgment. Allow me to laugh respectfully. I shall await it resolutely, for I have known what is worse, the judgment of men. For them, no extenuating circumstances; good intention is ascribed even to crime. . . . All dunces, all punished, let's spit on one another and—hurry!—toward discomfort! Each tries to spit first, that's all. I'll tell you a big secret, *mon cher.* Don't wait for the Last Judgment. It takes place every day.

The narrator discovers *that he must submit and realize his guilt.* People stop talking about pity only to prove themselves more pitiless: "It's just that no one is ever acquitted any more." The true torture: not just to be judged *but to be judged without law.* Hence this display:

No. I used to talk through my hat quite enough in the past. Now my words have a purpose. They have the purpose, obviously, of silencing the laughter, of avoiding judgment personally; though there is apparently no escape. Is not the great thing that stands in the way of our escaping it the fact that we are the first to condemn ourselves? Therefore it is essential to begin by extending the condemnation to all, without distinction, in order to thin it out at the start. No excuses ever, for anyone; that's my principle at the outset. I deny the good intention, the respectable mistake, the indiscretion, the extenuating circumstance.

A surprising dialectic, which re-creates in ironic mood the legerdemain that Camus indulges in at the end of *L'Homme Révolté* (The Rebel) making an arbitrary appeal to the Mediterranean spirit. Furthermore, it seems that the somber humor in his present demonstration accentuates its seriousness. Albert Camus is seeking once more to resolve his contradictions, a serious enterprise if there ever was one, even though he chooses for it a tone of half-pleasantry and the guise of a philosophical tale.

Emile Henriot, although acknowledging the nobility of Camus, described *La Chute* as a *disgusting confession* and *degrading philosophy.* As for me, I am inclined to believe that, with the exception of certain picturesque exaggerations and intentional caricatures, we are to take the greater part of our author's remarks literally. His somewhat strained irony confirms this interpretation, according to my way of thinking. It is true that I see nothing disgusting, still less degrading, quite the contrary, in these observations which go from the gloomy to the hopeless. It seems to me, for example, that a page like this one, which I think it useful to cite in its entirety, is made up of precise allusions to facts:

Once my attention was aroused, it was not hard for me to discover that I had enemies, first of all in my profession, and then in my social life. Among them were those I had obliged. Others I should have obliged. All that, after all, was natural, and I discovered it without too much grief. It was harder and more painful, on the other hand, to admit that I had enemies among people I hardly knew or didn't know at all. I had always thought, with the ingenuousness I have already illustrated to you, that those who didn't know me couldn't resist liking me if they came to know me. Not at all! I encountered hostility especially among those who knew me only at a distance without my knowing them myself. Doubtless they suspected me of living fully, given up completely to happiness; and that cannot be forgiven. The look of success, when it is worn in a certain way, would infuriate a jackass. Then again, my life was full to bursting, and for lack of time I used to refuse many advances. Then I would forget my refusals, for the same reason. But those advances had been made me by people whose lives were not full and who, for that very reason, would remember my refusals.

The bitterness is less important here than the chagrin. We think of Maurice Barrès once more and of that *tardy, bitter, sincere* confidence reported by Henri Mondor: "If something is true, it calls for the pursuit of a certain perfect note which must be detached from within us, composed and expressed. If something is false, we say there is pleasure in notoriety." The hero of *La Chute*, whom we must identify with his creator in this respect, does not pretend to be indifferent to incomprehension and jealousy. He confesses his anxiety at feeling that these hostile reactions are at times justified; certainly not unpardonable jealousy but what we call incomprehension, comprehension different from our own: "As for me, the injustice was even greater: I was condemned for past successes. For a long time I had lived in the illusion of a general agreement, whereas, from all sides, judgments, arrows, mockeries rained upon me, inattentive and smiling. The day I was alerted I became lucid; I received all the wounds at the same time and lost my strength all at once. The whole universe then began to laugh at me." The tone here is that of Nietzsche.

These wounds inflicted from outside would be of little consequence if they did not reveal a secret evil in the narrator, known by him alone, a momentary act of cowardice for which he will never forgive himself and with which he remains obsessed: one day, a young woman had drowned herself not very far from him without his coming to her aid. In the absence of a point of reference, the critic must remain discreet here and not try to imagine what personal matter Albert Camus wished to express by this allusion to a fault which, from the evidence at hand, he did not commit and which one ought to attribute to his protagonist alone. No doubt this invented trait is there in place of a real one. Perhaps Albert Camus simply wanted to suggest the feeling of guilt that he had always had and which we all share. Fortunate is the man who thinks he can protest: "I am not at all convinced and I declare myself innocent of all the dirty things that have been imputed to me and the lack of conscience that on principle I am supposed to have. . . . And, by saying this, I am simply defending man, whom our somber doctors call indefensible."

In *La Chute* Albert Camus renounces the paradoxical and arbitrary optimism of his preceding books, the hope born of despair to which *Le Mythe de Sisyphe, La Peste* (The Plague) and *L'Homme révolté* testify. He does not deny his past attempts to tailor to man's measure the enormity that overwhelms him, but he relaxes for a moment, to catch his breath a bit, and mildly complain. Not so happy as to want to prove his happiness to himself in order to be less uncomfortable, Sisyphus, suffering and in despair, looks for a change of position so that his grief may be lulled to sleep or dismissed. Thus, *La Chute* came into being, the most beautiful book that Albert Camus has written since *Le Mythe de Sisyphe*. Since *L'Etranger* (The Stranger), too, the real subject of which was already the guilt of the innocent. To make it comprehensible, Camus chose the perpetrator of a murder, simplification that first allowed the guilt to be admissible (Meursault had committed murder), and then the innocence (he had not wanted the murder; it was, in a way, committed independently of himself, through too much sun and drunkenness, he tried to explain to his judges, who, of course, could not accept such an excuse). To tell the truth, even though Meursault did not really feel responsible for this event, he considered himself no less guilty, but his guilt existed even before the crime. From the very first pages of the book, when he is at his dead mother's wake, he suddenly notices the inmates of the asylum, gathered with him around the corpse: "For a moment I had the ridiculous impression that they were there to judge me." Later, but still before the tragedy, he thinks about a moment when he wanted to justify himself for an infraction of a rule of decorum: "It didn't mean anything. At any rate, one is always a little at fault." Meursault of *L'Etranger* could have said as Clamence of *La Chute* did: "I have never been really sincere and enthusiastic except when I indulged in sports, and in the army, when I acted in plays we put on for our own amusement. In both cases there was a rule of the game, which was not serious but which we enjoyed taking as if it were. Even now, the Sunday matches in an overflowing stadium, and the theater, which I loved passionately, are the only places in the world where I feel innocent." But here it is Albert Camus and no longer Jean-Baptiste Clamence who is speaking. (We know his fondness for the theater and sports.)

The didactic end of *L'Etranger* does not fit in with the rest of the book. What sudden spiritual agility appears in this man of lazy and uncouth thought. The hero's speech becomes too well articulated. The author has taken his place and is speaking in his name, defending a thesis that he constantly propounds in various guises: man's victory, proclaimed by him in the midst of his defeat. This artifice, a moving one, is a weakness of the novel that reveals the moral strength of the novelist. This man *alone* is the man of *La Chute* again— but the man who, in *La Chute*, explains himself from the first pages with a facility of elocution which, this time, is in keeping with his character. The author wanted Clamence to be even more forsaken and defenseless than the criminal of *L'Etranger,* his crimes appearing at the same time less serious but more difficult because they were lived through and assumed with derision. The laugh which Jean-Baptiste Clamence hears one evening is that of his contempt for himself. We do not like him any less in spite of himself, and all the more in that he seems lost to a greater extent; there is no dawn to justify him like the one in which Meursault will die on the guillotine. "To drain the last drop, for me to feel less alone, there remained my wish that there be many spectators on the day of my execution and that they greet me with cries of hate." These last words of *L'Etranger*, a little too spontaneous, herald the cruel and sardonic tone of *La Chute*. This "irresponsible *minus habens*" about whom a critic curiously spoke, the Meursault of *L'Etranger*, understood that there is no way out for a man doomed to death. Such is the true sense of these *what's-the-use's* of an individual for whom all gestures are the same, in as much as none of them helps. It is from a keen intelligence that his apparent unintelligence proceeds—and from a fundamental nobility, his refusal to play a game fixed in advance. No doubt *La Chute* will become clearer with the years and no one in ten years will be able to say of Jean-Baptiste Clamence, as I heard someone assure me, that he is a good-for-nothing bum.

It is instructive to see Christ evoked in these two books, of which one marks the point of departure and the other an already distant stage of a thought moving toward its fulfillment. Christ is denied in both, but in *La Chute* with less violence, with regret, almost with nostalgia. Not that the unbeliever has any doubts. Camus now feels sufficiently sure of himself to evoke Christ without blasphemy and even with a kind of complicity. It is not the God that he loves in Jesus (since he does not believe in God), but the man who, even he, was not altogether innocent:

The children of Judea massacred while his parents were taking him to a safe place—why did they die if not on his account? He had not wanted it, surely. Those blood-spattered soldiers, those infants cut in two, filled him with horror. But, given the man he was, I am sure he could not forget them. And as for that sadness that can be felt in his every act, wasn't it the incurable melancholy of a man who heard night after night the voice of Rachel weeping for her children and refusing all comfort? The lamentation would rend the night, Rachel would call her children who had been killed for him, and he was was still alive!

But it is above all the Christ of "Wherefore hast thou forsaken me?" that Camus salutes: "And he was not superhuman, you can take my word for it. He cried aloud in his agony and that's why I love him, my friend who died without knowing." Already in *L'Etranger,* despite the vehemence of Meursault's refusal, we sense in Camus the nostalgia of Salvation. The police magistrate, a believer, was not presented as antipathetic, in spite of his excesses and clumsiness. At times, even, it is a part of Camus which is expressed by his voice, the Camus who would have liked to believe but could not (faith is a temptation to which it may be nobility not to yield) :

[He asked me] if I believed in God. I answered no. He sat down in indignation. He said to me that it was impossible, that all men believed in God, even those who turned away from his face. That was his conviction, and if he ever had to doubt it, his life would have no more sense. "Do you," he exclaimed, "want my life not to have any sense?" In my opinion, that was none of my business, and I told him so. But across the table he was already shoving the Christ under my eyes and yelling in an irrational way: "I am a Christian."

Eventually, the judge accepted the fact of the unbelief of the accused and calmed down: "That is all for today, *Monsieur Antéchrist.*" We read in *La Chute:* "On dead innocence the judges swarm, the judges of all species, those of Christ and those of Antichrist, who are the same anyway, reconciled in their discomfort. One mustn't blame everything exclusively on the Christians. The others are involved too." Albert Camus does not dissociate himself from the general guilt. That redeeming *communal spirit* of *La Peste* is now that of solitary yet united men, all accomplices and all unfortunate, all judges and all judged. That is where the profession of judge-penitent comes from, the profession that Jean-Baptiste Clamence claims as his own: "In as much as every judge some day ends up as a penitent, one has to travel the road in the opposite direction and practice the profession of penitent to be able to end up as a judge":

The essential lies in being able to permit oneself everything, even if, from time to time, one has to profess vociferously one's own infamy. I permit myself everything again, and without laughter this time. I haven't changed my way of life; I continue to love myself and to make use of others. Only, the confession of my crimes allows me to begin again lighter in heart and to taste a double enjoyment, first of my nature and secondly of a charming repentance.

Camus emphasizes the ignominy of Jean-Baptiste Clamence to the point of absurdity, just as he exaggerated Meursault's lucidity at the end of *L'Etranger*. Where this author is least successful is in his endings. We have already pointed out the ultimate artifice of *L'Homme révolté*, where Camus, hoping to escape from the contradictions of his subject, calls with euphoric seriousness on the joyous Mediterranean to impart confidence and joy again. This sleight of hand by the writer, manifested by an artist who wants to complete his work and sew it up, is embarrassing in both cases. It is a little less so perhaps in *La Chute* by reason of the caricaturing comments of Camus: on the other hand, it is a little more so, too, because of the masochism suddenly evidenced by an author who had, up to this point, treated himself so much better—too well perhaps. If he goes to the extreme of making Clamence odious, isn't it done with the ulterior motive of compromising himself along with his hero? Albert Camus no longer wants to be taken for someone else. He prefers to espouse the opinions of his judges, since, in fact, if he feels innocent on the points for which he is reproved, he knows he is guilty of others. Since there are no innocents, this is perhaps a subtle way of pleading not guilty in spite of everything. Each one of us must accommodate himself as best he can to the anxiety of life.

HENRI MICHAUX

"IF THE DOORS OF PERCEPTION WERE WASHED CLEAN, EVERY-thing would appear to man as it actually is: infinite." This sentence of Blake's gave Aldous Huxley the title for his book on mescaline. As he had already noted in his work *Ends and Means*, the world of our daily existence is the resultant of our insufficiencies. As a remedy for those shortcomings, the author of *The Doors of Perception* recommends the use of mescaline, the active ingredient of the peyote used by the Indians of Mexico. Before Aldous Huxley, as we have seen, Antonin Artaud brought this drug into literature in *Au Pays des Tarahumaras*.

One day in May, 1953, Aldous Huxley took four decigrams of mescaline. Two witnesses assisted him with a tape re-corder to register the oral results of the experiment. If this document in sound served as a point of departure for the writing of his study, there is no indication to that effect. It is true that its transcription into writing was impractical. On this point, however, and although he found himself *in great difficulty before the wall of typography,* Henri Michaux did better than Aldous Huxley, after his ingestions of mescaline—from the first one, limited to three quarters of a one-decigram capsule, to that in which, by mistake, he swallowed six such capsules at once, and other occasions. To the elaborate account given in *Misérable Miracle* and *L'Infini turbulent* (The Turbulent Infinity) he has added information gathered elsewhere from original notes.

Aldous Huxley, after his recovery from his prudent incursions into the enchanted domain of this artificial paradise, concluded that mescaline enabled one *to know contemplation at its peak.* This sudden modesty in spiritual ambition is surprising on the part of a scholar whom we know to be preoccupied with the most diverse and noble forms of mysticism. Master Eckhart and St. John of the Cross are neighbors with Lao-Tse and Sri Aurobindo in his work *The Perennial Philosophy.* Although he was careful to indicate that he would not try to match the dazzling effects of the drug, mescaline, "with the conscious awareness of the ultimate aim and end of human life: the Illumination, the Vision of Beatitude," the author of *The Doors of Perception* is none the less led to suggest "for those for whom piety is not sufficient" [*sic*] the use of that *free grace* which an ideal drug provides. Mescaline comes very close, according to him, to what is required of such a product.

This is the concept, dear to Huxley, of a *substitute for religion* such as he has already defined in *The Dumbest Animal.* Quoting, in *The Doors of Perception,* Philippe de Félice and his essay: *Poisons sacrés, Ivresses divines,* (Sacred Poisons, Divine Intoxications), Huxley writes that if Christian rites are incompatible with intoxication, even religious intoxication, "it does not hurt the distillers but is very bad for Christianity." Are there not many men and women "who desire the transcendence of the ego and would be happy to find it in a church?" Also the ideal communion exists (you may think you are dreaming!) thanks to a sect of Indians affiliated with the native American church and for whom, Aldous Huxley writes without any trace of irony or reprobation, "slices of peyote replace the sacramental bread and wine."

As the title he gave his book indicates, Henri Michaux was not satisfied with these cheap ecstasies. After *Misérable Miracle* came *L'Infini turbulent*, which ends with this lucid phrase: "ill-deserved infinity." From the very beginning, he was on guard against being duped. It was not even a question of having an open mind, friendly or not. *He is against it:* "Mescaline and I have often been more at odds than together. I was shaken, broken, but I didn't give in." The spectacle, he found, was empty glitter, a fairyland, but silly. At a hundred images per second the *inharmonious mescaline* "develops foolishly." Idiot, ape. "Not a God, a howling monkey." He is *ashamed and furious.* Where Huxley sings and is delighted, Michaux sings another tune: "I was the fireworks who despised the fireworks-maker."

Everything becomes different when, because of an error in dosage, a volcanic eruption takes place after the Bengal Lights. In the brutal perdition of his whole being, Henri Michaux keeps enough consciousness to bring back from that abyss a few invaluable notes. But, there again, he reduces the cataclysm to its human proportions. It is not to contemplation's peak that mescaline takes him, but to the borders of madness. Having entered what should indeed be called the rationale of irrationality, he lived and understood dementia from the inside. It is a different logic, but just as forceful, and we accept it for the first time because for the first time it is explained to us. There is no doubt that psychiatrists can learn much from *Misérable Miracle* and *L'Infini turbulent*.

Knowing at last the how, if not the why, of certain dementias, perhaps they can treat them better. Henri Michaux went from the confines of furious madness to the more harmless but just as painful ones of persecution mania. In doing this, he rediscovered, in an overstimulated but recognizable form, certain traits of his nature with which his books had familiarized us. He shows a sort of obsession to murder, for example: the aggressiveness of frustrated organisms which attack only because they are afraid. He looks like a raving maniac: "I would have frightened a killer." We recognize the perverse impulses which he has the greatest difficulty in resisting, "insatiable, which ten murders and as many acts of arson would not have satisfied." He finds it suddenly impossible to tolerate anyone else. We read in *Misérable Miracle*:

A man with his back to me, toward whom my feelings were actually indifferent, he is the one that I was tempted to throw into the water, tempted to the point that for several days I preferred to keep away from the Seine. . . . But some time after that, —— having telephoned and in disagreement with me . . . I was seized with a moment of fury, a fury, a fury which I didn't know where to hurl and get rid of, an insane fury, an altogether new fury. . . . It was his person that was my target, and more than his person, that part of his quintessence that was the most opposite to mine, and which I would have liked, not to harm but to obliterate, definitely abolish, essence by essence, against which I could never be angry enough, contrary enough, antagonistic enough. . . . All day long I had to make an effort to divert my attention from the intolerable thought of our coexistence on earth.

In *Ici, Poddema* (This Is Poddema), one of the universes of *Ailleurs* (Elsewhere), Henri Michaux has us meet some creatures in whom exist a hundred uncommitted crimes. Here is one, for example: "Thanks to that same inner slaughter, he maintained himself in happy activity until an advanced age. Furthermore, they leave him in peace, being careful never to show him his dossier, for, either he is hardly aware of his condition or else he believes innocently that everyone is similarly a killer." But speaking in his own name, and calm this time, terribly calm, Henri Michaux notes in *Ecuador:*

That Brazilian Jew who was supposed to take us to Iquitos, I greatly regret not having been able to kill him. No opportunity could be found to do away with him without killing the boy who was with him as well. One stormy night on the river we were almost cut adrift. My companion and I had the same thought, our hands on our revolvers. If the canoe slips her moorings, we blow his brains out. We were in perfect agreement about it.

Of course, we must take into account Henri Michaux's particular brand of humor. Nevertheless, nothing, not even drugs, can make a man different from what he is. What comes to the surface has existed already, at any rate in a latent state. If one wishes to draw conclusions of a philosophical nature, we are dealing here with a somewhat demoniacal reality. "The demon," writes Michaux in *Misérable Miracle.* "Why never the angel? Isn't there any drug for angels? It seems not."

Henri Michaux takes the precaution of pointing out at the end of *Misérable Miracle:* "To amateurs of one-sided perspective the temptation might arise of henceforth judging the whole of my writings as the work of a drug addict. I am sorry. I am more of the water-drinking type." And he specifically states that he uses no stimulant, and, for years, not even coffee, tobacco, or tea. "Once in a great while some wine, and very little." Nothing could be more studied and contrived than the fantastic tales of Michaux: on a basis *other* than that of reality as we see it, he constructs with a great deal of logic the elements of universes and societies that are different from but no more absurd than those of our cities and planets. Consequently, it is impossible to attribute these controlled divagations to some drug. He adds, to assuage his conscience: "I forgot. I must have tried, twenty-five or more years ago, ether seven or eight times, laudanum once, and twice, repulsive alcohol." Even though Michaux's books retain little trace of these experiments, we do not lose sight of them. In particular, the ether and laudanum are reported in *Ecuador*.

To these should be added opium, about which the author says in the same work: "A round word which would cover almost all of my idea of Asia and which filled my youth with a real obsession: *Opium*. I know you now . . . and you are not one of my friends. This perfection without outside strength is nothing to me. Rather I prefer ether, which is more Christian, which uproots a man." An admitted obsession. A desired uprooting. (We find in a poem in *Face aux verrous* [Facing the Bolts] the story of *operation uprooting*.) So it was not by chance that, thirty years later, Henri Michaux tried mescaline, then hashish, came back again to mescaline and finally wrote *Misérable Miracle* and *L'Infini turbulent*. He mentions in one of his *Idées de traverse* (Side Ideas) some horses who take drugs:

Thus they were not so pleased with it either, with this world, the everlasting fixedness of everything always in its place and the fine equilibrium of four hooves. . . . He [the horse] then also loves images, dreams, the ungluing of the ego, the liquidation of his faithful organs (bores you stiff how faithful they are!) and of the ground (so faithful, also).

This old excerpt was later included in *Passages*, a title which is a kind of travel guide. In *Ailleurs* we get back to the *Voyage en Grande Garabagne*, where we read that "by diversified, infinitesimal and strong perfumes" the Emanglons seek "to obtain new horizons, to take trips," a nostalgia for which has always tormented Henri Michaux. Was that why he went and visited the Ecuadorians, the Indians of the Amazon, then the Hindus, the Chinese, the Japanese, and the Malays [read the splendid *Un Barbare en Asie* (A Barbarian in Asia)]? One might think that these stories of hooved beasts had antedated the imaginary voyages. Actually, they are contemporary, as a text from *Passages* informs us. His Emanglons, his Magi and the famous Plume himself were all buffer-characters arising out of his travels where almost everything hurt him: "As soon as I had found a character (and had *fallen back on him*) I was relieved of embarrassment, of suffering (at least the roughest part, the most intolerable). Now it is your turn! That is why the foreign country was an opportunity, a provocation of characters to whom I turned matters over from then on, those of enjoying or suffering from strange and hostile people and things."

The idea of *stranger*, already mentioned in the essay on Camus, is also one of the fundamental elements of Henri Michaux's mythology. See for example, "L'Etranger parle" (The Stranger Speaks) in *Face aux verrous*. Whatever is different attracts him and at the same time frightens him.

But habit, far from saving him, immediately drags him too far in the opposite direction. Even if he is no longer annoyed and hurt by the outer world, Michaux continues to suffer none the less. But then it is the excessive amount of banality that disturbs him. From the first pages of the travel diary *Ecuador,* he describes the ennui of *this damned planet with the little of everything that it possesses*: "There are some regions where it is so well expurgated of every surprise that one wonders where our true place is and of what other globe we are the miserable suburb." But the more one changes places, the less hope remains of really being abroad: "This earth is rinsed of its exoticism. If in a hundred years we have not found the way to be in contact with another planet (but we shall succeed), humanity is lost." Hence his escape into imagination, where he reintroduces at the same time the strangeness which hurts him and the desire for another, more subtle, poetic, and rich non-existent strangeness, the lack of which is also painful to him. He seeks dreamed experiences which he will recount with invented words in so far as they are indescribable: "The Murnes: pretentious, gulloping, gobish, ectraboot, famed for their stupidity . . ." [*Voyage en Grande Garabagne*] "Why travel when a rhyme leveled a mountain for him, when an adjective populated a country, when an assonance made the entire earth shake?" ["Les Poètes Voyagent" (The Poets Are Traveling), in *Passages*]

But imagination is slow, and it is reticent and restive. How can one escape the temptation to influence it from without? We read in *Passages*:

Thinking! I would rather act upon my being-machine (and thinking-machine) so as to be in a position to be able to think with novelty, to have possibilities of really new thought. In that sense I should have liked to have done some work in experimental thought. I am aware of it, it is above all an "I should have liked to."

This note was written in 1950. When did the mescaline cruises and storms take place? A few years after, no doubt. But no matter. The interesting thing is that he realized this wish, that he really did work in experimental thought. The adventure in hashish forced this cry from him (it is no longer a matter of making a vow but an avowal):

I become bored quickly nowadays while traveling. So much that has already been seen and a certain aging, even in the eye, perhaps! Whatever may be the cause, enjoyment had returned, its very self, alone and sufficient. With an intense look full of wonderment, I touched palm trees and rocks with my tentacles. [*Misérable Miracle*]

We are tempted to see an act of negligence in the error in dosage from which he was to make a voyage to the end of the mescaline night. It was an experiment in madness, as we have already pointed out. But as far back as *Ecuador* he spoke of "an attack which madness sought to undertake upon him." It is moving to discover throughout his work more or less precise premonitions of the *great ordeal of the mind* ("the worst moment of his existence"), that he owed to that excessive intake of mescaline: a disintegration of thought the horror of which exceeds all that one can express and which nevertheless he tries to tell, and which he does tell in his poet's language. In *Ecuador,* the fatigue and fevers of a frightful expedition inspire a poem where we find:

> Despair is sweet,
> Sweet to the point of vomiting.
> And I am afraid, afraid,

When my very marrow begins to tremble,
Oh! I am afraid, I am afraid
I can't stand it any more, I can hardly stand it any more.

Again we read in *Mes propriétés* (My Properties) : "But a storm blew up, and the roots, to resist the increasing wind, bored into me—a mere trifle—but they went on to hook so deeply into me that it was worse than death." Several poems of *Face aux verrous* recall with such intensity the data of *Misérable Miracle* and *L'Infini turbulent* that one wonders (the dates are unavailable) if they are not also a commentary. Notably *Mouvements* "written about signs representing movements" could well be related to the vibratory sketches reproduced in the aforementioned works:

Signs
not of roofs, tunics or palaces
not of archives or a dictionary of learning
but of twisting, of violence, of jostling
but of kinetic envy . . .

Signs of stampede, of pursuit, of frenzy, signs for the shape of unbridled demons:

Signs not for retreat to the rear
but "to cross the Line" better at every moment
signs not as one copies
but as one pilots
or, barging through unwitting, as one is piloted . . .

But there is some evidence antedating *Misérable Miracle* which shows us this uprooting and this perdition already linked to the drug. We find it in *Ecuador*:

In front of me is the man with the ether bottle and he is
pouring.
Ah! That's all Infinity is! Ah! meanwhile the fog drinks
me in . . .

Infinite . . . infinite all the same.
Infinite error of the one who would think that . . .
because, it is only, that I . . .
The speed . . .
The distance . . .
The water . . .

No, it is not infinity. We have already said that the author of *Misérable Miracle* is not unaware of it. But, if he tried the experiment once more, in spite of his past disillusions, it was because despite everything he was hoping for a revelation.

From Michel Leiris we passed without haitus to Samuel Beckett. And it is back to Samuel Beckett that Henri Michaux leads us. I mean: to the same universe of terror and ice. The author of *Ecuador* already has spoken of his *faithful larvas and phantoms*. And here is *L'Espace aux ombres* (The Space in the Shadows) :

At the moment of their arrival, they are going to understand, they understand. In vain, they wanted to hope! Their life will have been only a reprieve. Here, surely, they will be dominated. Impossible to keep the mask on, to find a new one. They are at bay. Woe, woe to them, since their apparition, hunted by the *Birds of Prey of the Invisible*. [*Face aux verrous*]

A book of Michaux' which we have already mentioned is called *Mes propriétés*. How can one help thinking of what Beckett calls his *possessions*? "These properties are my only properties and I have dwelt here since my childhood and I can say that very few people own poorer ones." Michaux acknowledges that he wrote this book as a form of hygiene, for his health. Certain beings, he tells us, are so seriously infected "that in order not to founder they are obliged to have recourse to entirely new ideas." The only imagination found in *Mes propriétés* is that of the *incapacity to conform.* "An operation within reach of everyone and which, it seems, ought to be so profitable to the weak, to the sick and sickly, to children, to the oppressed and inadapted of all kinds." [Postface to *La Nuit remue* (The Night Moves)] In the same way he points out that the poems in his work: *Epreuves, Exorcismes,* (Ordeals, Exorcisms) "were not exactly written out of hatred for this or that, but to deliver himself from seizures." And here is another passage from *Mes propriétés* which is again in the tone of Beckett: .

If I always changed into animal form, as a last resort I would in the end get used to it . . . but I'm things too (and even things would be bearable), but I'm such artificial and impalpable combinations. What a to-do when I was changed into lightning! . . . Oh! if I could only die once and for all! But no, I'm always found good for some new being. . . . There are so many animals, so many plants, so many minerals. And I have already been everything so many times. But these experiments don't help me. Becoming ammonium hydrochlorate again for the thirty-second time, I still have a tendency to behave like arsenic, and, changed once more into a dog, my night-bird habits always show up. Only rarely do I see something without experiencing this very special feeling . . . *Ah yes, I've been* THAT . . . I don't remember exactly, I feel it.

This Kafkaian theme of metamorphosis is one of his *leitmotivs.* "When I begin to bud, to form paws, even very incomplete ones, even some sort of stumps, that is when I begin again to enter the road of deliverance." Career suggestions for himself include a pigeon, a leaf, a young girl, a hedge, a pebble, a cloud, and even a sea of clouds. [*Passages*] He is not only the ants but their path. He magnifies himself irresistibly, then contracts himself to the point of being contained in a teacup. [*Mes propriétés*] "When your foot is at the end of a long hangar, what a job to bring it back! What a big job! [*La Vie dans les plis* (Life in Its Habits)] Hashish and mescaline revive for Michaux the games of former days. With hashish, human beings often seem small, eight inches being in general the maximum, but it is not "the enormous crowd of microbe-men of mescaline." Mescaline, moreover, also has a tendency to elongate, making everything more slender, a phenomenon less common where hashish is concerned. In "Arriver à se reveiller" (Waking Up), one of the pieces in *Passages,* we find some bones about a hundred meters in length, in places almost thread-shaped. Here, taken from the same pages, is a sentence which could be Beckett's, which is pure Beckett, without there being, of course, the least bit of imitation or even the least influence, that is to say, direct influence, but only a kind of similar original impulse and identical experience, and something like the respect for the same rule of the game: "Then, in silence and exhaustion, I return to my paralysis, the only and undeniable reality."

Let us leave aside the differences. Humor, for example, humor, in particular, which we have already indicated in the creator of *Un Certain Plume.* Let us get to the essential. No break whatsoever in tone or even in background between a Franz Kafka and an Albert Camus, a Michel Leiris and a Samuel Beckett; to an even more striking degree between a Samuel Beckett and an Henri Michaux. If a whole race of writers speak the same language today, it is because they are releasers of the same secret. Even though they only know their own drama and discuss only themselves, it is a matter of a common curse and a search for a common salvation. To such an extent that the exegeses of the writers in question are themselves interchangeable. Most critics re-write the same article indefinitely. Only the proper nouns change, while those of Joyce and Kafka are found from one text to the other. The same holds true for a certain dramatic and art criticism today. This is the cause of the monotony in present-day French letters and commentary on it, and of that impression of intelligence turning toward emptiness. This is also the source of inevitable injustices, as such a perspective arbitrarily neglects all works which are not in accord with it. Authors who are not decoded by this special template are considered by the best critics as devoid of mystery, and, therefore, of interest. A reaction of the thermidorian type will follow one day or another, just as excessive itself. It will be a question of recovering a sense of proportion in lucidity and calm, that is to say, to begin from this moment to revise values and especially non-values (or those claimed as such). This does not mean that one must deny the talent, or even the greatness, of writers like Antonin Artaud, Henry Miller, Michel Leiris, Samuel Beckett, Georges Bataille, Albert Camus, Henri Michaux. But one can also, as seriously and in as fruitful a way, meditate on Georges Simenon, for example, and write about him.

GEORGES SIMENON

GEORGES SIMENON DOES WITH HIS CHARACTERS THE SAME thing that his character Chief Inspector Maigret does with the criminals he is after: he puts himself in their boots, identifying himself with them in order to reconstruct the chain of their reasoning and emotions. In fact, all his heroes resemble him.

Therefore, there is perhaps no writer who confesses more intimate secrets to us than this author of detective and popular fiction whose fertile imagination is justly famous.

The stranger his creatures' actions are, the more Georges Simenon depends on them to express what is important to him without betraying himself. This is disclosed by a certain style and the indiscriminate repetition of references that have a personal significance. Of course, the fact that we find the same mischievous, redheaded twins on the same broken-down bicycles in *The Watchmaker of Everton* and

The Black Ball is of no great importance. It just happened to be an image that impressed Georges Simenon. Other duplications have more value. A toothache for example, reappears in *The Watchmaker of Everton* and *The Accomplices*: a childhood memory, an allusion to a painful and yet delightful crisis that "made him accept a superior reality in which everything took on a sharper reality."

Again, we notice the frequent repetition in Simenon's work of the relationships of father to son and son to father. "Wasn't it this time that he had sworn to himself to resemble his father?" This little sentence from *The Watchmaker of Everton* is a personal avowal (for which the autobiographical origins may be found in *Pedigree*).

In almost all of the new-style Simenons we see "strange and very subtle bonds" being woven among his people [*New Man in Town*], subtle messages that are immediately identified, if not always understood. Such is the enigmatic glance of Mrs. Katz in *Belle*, "an imperceptible movement to explain something" to the one who is erroneously accused of murder: an appeal, a signal, whose meaning neither he nor the reader will ever know. From father to son, it is still more precise. Dave, the watchmaker of Everton, has in his mind's eye the red earth of Virginia that his runaway child sees at the same moment. If, at the peak of his own distress, he smiles, "it does not signify anything precise, only a kind of contact with Ben, down there." In the end, the father becomes so accustomed to this strong presence born of absence that he no longer has as great a need as in the past for the physical presence of his son. But the child misunderstands, breaks off the contact, or else is unaware of the common wave length. Finally, Dave, at last in his son's presence, assumes a facial expression, a sort of message, which he tries in vain to communicate: "He would have liked so much for Ben to look at him and understand all he had been through." [*The Watchmaker of Everton*] In the same way, but this time with nefarious intent, the depraved mother of the hero of *The Black Ball,* from far away, before dying, tries to entice her son out of the security and respectability that he has won for himself and his family: "If Louisa had really tried to signal to him she had failed, for never again in his life would he hunger after or breathe again the disgusting odor of the house on East 32nd Street, nor would his wife and children ever experience poverty either."

As he finds it difficult to please himself, Georges Simenon is no longer satisfied with current psychology. If he suggests more than he expresses, it is primarily, as Gilbert Sigaux has noted, because "the choice of a certain quality of silence is not a choice that leads to the elimination of problems but to stating them without recourse to speech." But it is also because these presentiments of truth, without being indescribable, are still too little known to make it possible for anyone who uncovers, and perhaps discovers them, to bring them out into the open. The subject of *Accomplices* is somewhat indecent, like the majority of the latest Simenon novels. What happened between the man and woman when the bus horn *screamed interminably* has its equivalent in *The Little Man from Archangel.* We shall have to return to the importance of sex in the work of Simenon, particularly in his recent books. But we must point out without further delay that the true boldness of the author of *Accomplices* is of a psychological order. The deeds of his heroes are nothing in comparison with the obscure ruminations from which they proceed. "What existed between them was on a different plane from ordinary life, life as it is known, as it is lived, as one wishes it to be. It was almost as though, at a given moment, without any apparent reason, they both exchanged a signal and escaped." Or again: "They were not lovers, they were, they had always been, two accomplices."

These quotations from *Accomplices* indicate the poles that most of Georges Simenon's recent novels oscillate between. This is particularly true of *The Little Man from Archangel*, our author's best story, I would say, except that I always think the best Simenon is what I have just finished reading. Jonas Milk, the humble bookseller, too, has gone beyond *a certain stage*. He, too, changes planes, passing over *to the other side*. "At a given moment in the morning, he could not say precisely which, and it was of no importance, a break had taken place. It was as if a thread had been cut, or, better, as if he had suddenly escaped from the law of gravity." Wrongly accused, he none the less is led to believe himself guilty, *but not in the way they thought*. These two themes, that of expatriation and that of *guilt*, are found not only in all of Simenon's works. We find them also in Michaux and in Albert Camus, in particular in *L'Etranger*. Georges Simenon is not imitating anyone, he is illustrating the common obsessions of his period. The following is a significant passage from a preface he wrote for a novel by Arthur Omré, *Traqué* (Man Hunt):

It was then that successive chance events taught me that, here and there, isolated people like myself were each in his own corner following parallel directions. This is something that I consider marvelous; the discovery that characters of Steinbeck, of Kafka, of Faulkner, and many others, born in Finland, Spain, or elsewhere, are marked with the same sign. What I believe I sense being born is a new conception of man, a new way to look at men. And because of this fact, it is the novel of tomorrow that is trying to find itself, that is groping, but that is being born. . . .

It is not we, it is Simenon himself who refers to Kafka, from whom we definitely cannot escape, no matter how hard we try to discover areas of modern literature where his prophetic shadow does not fall.

Most of Georges Simenon's characters have an acute sense of communal feeling. A Russian émigré and a Jew, Jonas Milk, "the little man from Archangel," always wants to become integrated into the French milieu of Berry, which he has known since childhood. Accepted by the inhabitants of his street as one of them, he is amazed to see himself denied and rejected at the first serious difficulty. In the same way, the professor in *Belle*, who is similarly suspected of a crime that he did not commit, feels himself excluded from the community. This Ashby is led to wonder, like Milk, whether he ever really was a part of it. "In his mind this was clear, the two thousand and some inhabitants of the locality constituted a whole; they were united not by a vague feeling of solidarity or duty but by bonds as rigid and complex as those that are the basis of great families." A whole of which he is no longer a part. Bonds which have been broken. Spencer Ashby has precisely the impression that Jonas Milk will experience later. Except for a few details, these lines from *Belle* could have been taken from *The Little Man from Archangel*: "They did not accuse him. They did not throw stones at him. They said nothing to him. Deep down, for years perhaps, had they not merely tolerated him? It was not his village. It was not his church. No family here knew his family and there were none of his ancestors in the cemetery; not a tomb, not a page in the parish register, bore his name." During the church service, they are all there around him like a faction. In unison, their songs "pour forth from the subconscious depth where they have their roots." He feels something like a void surrounding him and he is silent.

There exists in those American towns which Simenon describes as accurately as French towns, what he calls a religious geography. Higgins, the hero of *The Black Ball*, has unconsciously chosen his denomination in keeping with his social status. Those who are gathered with him in this church on Sunday have almost all had difficult childhoods. The strict atmosphere and the austerity reassure them. They could not adjust themselves to the pomp of the High Church to which most of the important people of the town belong.

This social geography is found with all its boundary lines clearly delineated in all public gatherings, in the town meetings, for example. Each member takes his place by instinct, the poorest in the rows farthest back. It is a projection which is as informative as the disposition of neighborhoods and their population. The intermediate group to which Higgins belongs keeps in the middle, as it should, and includes merchants, contractors, doctors, professors, teachers, and, finally, a few supervisory employees.

We always have, then, in the beginning, the comfort of settled lives. At the start of each novel the hero goes through his daily actions with carefree unconcern. There is no story of Georges Simenon's (and we see this once more in *The Little Man from Archangel*) in which there is not a *rite* or *routine*. The: "It had become a rite" of *The Burial of M. Bouvet* or the "It was the only unaccustomed detail" of *The Fate of the Malous* are found in almost every Simenon novel. One day comes the surprise of a doubt, then a new truth. Jonas Milk notices that he knows nothing about his wife, and perhaps about himself. When he hears about a disconcerting, crucifying opinion his wife has expressed about him, he is deeply wounded. Immediately, he completely loses interest in his plight. Even though he has proof of his innocence, he neglects it, gives up the game, and commits suicide. In various forms, all of Simenon's heroes experience this brutal *awakening.*

Thus, the judge in *The Witnesses,* at the start of a quite usual interrogation: "A dozen times, fourteen times to be exact, it had befallen him to play the role that he was playing today, but this was the first time that he felt uneasy, as if a veil had been stretched between him and reality or as if reality had become distorted. Or else was it the contrary, was it that this time the faces appeared to him in their harsh truth?" The universe stops being benevolent. Simenon notes in *The Black Ball:* "That happens especially when one has a fever, or else, on certain evenings, at sunset. The world about you, apparently so well organized, the new houses, the close-cropped lawns, the cars on the road, suddenly lose their solidity and their reassuring character. You look at your own children as if they were strangers, you think about your work and the position you have made for yourself in society as if they were a trap, if not a farce." The same surprise is Alavoine's, the doctor in *Letter to My Judge,* who experiences an uneasiness analogous to that of the man who lost his shadow:

There was a moment, very simply, when I began to look about me with different eyes, and I saw a city which seemed strange to me, a pretty city, very neat, very bright, very clean, a city where everyone greeted me with affability.

Why, then, did I have the sensation of a void? I began to look at my house, too, and I asked myself why it was my house. . . . I looked at Armande and I had to repeat to myself that she was my wife.

Why?

And those two little girls who called me Papa . . .

In short, for years I had lived without noticing it. . . .

I continued to go through the everyday motions. I was not unhappy, don't think that. But I had the impression of floundering
about in a void.

Thanks to his books, it would no doubt be possible to fix
the date of this experience, which every man has, to some
degree, sooner or later, with regard to Georges Simenon's
life. His vision of the world was changed by it, and his conception of fiction. It is a fundamental discovery for most of
his heroes; it occurs sometimes after the irremediable has
taken place, sometimes relatively early in their existence,
or sometimes when they have reached or even passed middle
age. "Is that what they call becoming a man? If it is, until
the age of forty-five he had remained a child." Such is the
conclusion of Higgins. This "self-made man" understood,
upon the occasion of the first serious reversal in his slow
and patient social ascent, that there is in the life of society a
rule of the game. "What is important is to conform to the
rule, of course, but one must realize that it is a game, otherwise one makes the position of others impossible." And his
own, too, of course. [*The Black Ball*] The hero of *The Time
of Anais* was ashamed *not to do as others do*. This feeling
different is at the source of the crime he has committed.
The psychiatrist, responsible for estimating the degree of
his guilt, asks him: "Will you try to define for me, in your
opinion, what the others do?" Bauche, the character in *The
Time of Anais*, answers: "They follow the rules, or rather
they make believe they do, for everybody cheats.". . . In
Red Lights there is also a gentleman who "for thirty-two
years, close to thirty-three, had been an honest man; he fol-

lowed the straight and narrow . . . , a good son, an honorable student, employee, husband, father of a family, owner of a house on Long Island; he had never violated any law, never appeared in court on a summons, and every Sunday morning he went to church with his family. He was a happy man. He lacked nothing." Comes the hour of lucidity and of revolt (at least by proxy):

So, you understand, they create rules which they call laws, and they call sin everything that frightens them in other people. That's the truth, old man! If they didn't tremble, if they were real men, they would not need police and courts, pastors and churches. . . .

From this comes one of two temptations: either throw up your hands, play no more, give up the game, that is, life, which is what we saw Jonas Milk do, or else try to take revenge on the rules. Those who are content with them and adapt to them receive, if they rise in the world, the reward of a sure social success. "The others have only to continue to grovel in obscurity until they get caught in the trap." Higgins of *The Black Ball* finds peace by becoming a man like the others. He justifiably avoids the hopeless solution of crime or suicide (crime, moreover, is very often, for Simenon's heroes, a form of suicide). It has a fascination to which so many other unfortunates end by succumbing, not only the little man from Archangel, but Bauche in *The Time of Anais* and Spencer Ashby in *Belle*. Higgins, too, is looking for what is called happiness: "Do you know, Doctor, anyone who is happy?" "It was not the correct word, but he understood. No word exists for what he meant: someone who is at peace with himself and who does not ask himself questions or else who has found the answers. It is even more complicated than that." [*The Black Ball*] Too humble to

imagine that he could give his young wife happiness, Jonas
Milk promises her, for lack of a better word, tranquillity.
It is never the exact expression; but they themselves understand; it even happens sometimes that a privileged person
understands them. A theme that runs through all Simenon's
works is the impossibility of explaining oneself. The whole
book happens to be written from the point of view of the
person who, oddly enough, delves into the reasons for irrationality. Thus in *The Watchmaker of Everton* we see the
father learn, little by little, to understand his son, until he
feels he shares the responsibility for the murder the son
has committed. The same is true of the judge in *The Witnesses*. There is not a novel of the new-style Simenon which
does not deal with this effort toward comprehension on the
part of an individual overwhelmed by the incomprehension
of others. "He tried to think about Fernande and immediately he perceived that it was the features of Anais that
were in his mind's eye, that it was her perfume that he
sniffed. And people were trying to understand! But why,
good God? How could they ever hope to do it?" [*The Time
of Anais*]

We have left the social for the metaphysical. A very big
word? Georges Simenon himself invites us to use it when he
writes about M. Monde: "He was lucid, but not with any
ordinary lucidity, not the kind that one talks about but, on
the contrary, about which one blushes the next day, perhaps
because it gives to what is considered banal the grandeur
that poets and religions bestow on them." Once awakened
from his spiritual narcosis and brought back to his senses as
naturally, as surely, as he had left them, this gentleman who
had remained logical even in his derangement feels relieved: "He had no more phantoms, no more darkness, and

looked into your eyes with a cool serenity." [*The Flight of M. Monde*] Jonas Milk also has this peace and lucidity at the moment of his death.

Simenon's new-style novels convey the same impression of mystery, not just of the detective, but of the human story. The great secret of Kafka, like that of Camus and Simenon, is that there are no innocents. "Why, being guilty of nothing, did he have a sensation of guilt? In the light that prevailed at that moment, with the snow already losing its whiteness, the sky overcast, it was impressive to see the cunning-faced doctor hold the doorknob with an air of ushering Ashby into his own house as if into a kind of poorly lit court." [*Belle*] Similarly Jonas Milk "experienced the need to defend himself when he had done nothing." "Later he was to ask himself why, from that moment on, he had acted like a guilty man."

From the impossibility of understanding others stems the impossibility of judging them. If no one is completely innocent, no one is really guilty either. Most of Georges Simenon's accused people feel unjustly treated. That is what the hero of *Accomplices* thinks, first in regard to the refinements of his sexual life, then in regard to the catastrophe that comes from them. "Above all, he needed to prove to himself that it was they (she and he) who were right, that it was their right and that there was nothing degrading or guilty in the pleasure that they gave each other. . . . Didn't they now have the appearance of two cursed souls? Yet Lambert was persuaded of their innocence, that is what he wanted to shout to everyone, without hope of making himself understood." In all Simenon's recent novels (and again in *The Little Man from Archangel*) there is a desire for sexual justification concerning a woman much younger than the man who loves her. "Was Moriat aware of that drama also? We are not vicious, neither he nor I, no more than we are ambitious, but who will admit it except the few who bear the sign themselves? . . ." [*In Case of Emergency*]

Even the murderer in *The Time of Anais* finds only one sentence to express his case exactly: "I am an honest man."

The interrogation by the police, then that of the police magistrate, even though it is more subtle, seem to him *beside the point* and to proceed from so elementary a psychology that, like Jonas Milk and so many other Simenon characters, he soon stops trying to make himself understood. "It is not exactly that. I am going to try to explain it to you," he says at first. Then he stops talking, sure that there is nothing he can do, that he is doomed to be not simply the only one who understands but the only one who tries to understand. In a similar vein, Alavoine, the author of the *Letter to My Judge*, is silent throughout his whole trial. He could not explain to the jurors nor to the judge that he had actually freed the woman he had killed. A certain over-stimulated and almost insane form of love not only abolishes death but presupposes it and actually brings it about. The more Martine is his, the more Alavoine feels the need to absorb her. "She had become so much a part of his being that he no longer distinguished between them." If he kills her, it is so that she may become even more completely his. Henceforth, "Martine and I are together, Judge. . . ." She had consented to her death and he could no longer not kill her, since he could not bear that part of her inadmissible, ineffaceable personality of former times should subsist: the one that didn't know him and that he still did not know. But how is this to be explained?

Without taking into account that it would have meant playing their game, giving them what they wanted for their peace of mind more than for peace of conscience, for the sake of an example, for the honor of the bourgeois world to which each and every one of us belongs. Immediately my colleagues would have signed the certificate of insanity which, even today, they are still striving to legitimize and which would straighten out so many things.

Nothing, then, can be hoped for from the judges on behalf of the guilty "for it is their business to support the world's ideas." [*The Time of Anais*] One judge, however, puts himself in the place of the accused, and that is the one in *The Witnesses*, who was obsessed from the first morning of the trial by the sudden realization that "it is impossible for one human being to understand another." Still satisfied with the record the night before, now he could no longer attach the slightest value to the various bits of testimony. "Each time he heard an affirmation made, he wanted to ask: What does he know about it? Or else: What does that prove?" Another man, already convicted, begins his long missive thus: "Your Honor, I would like someone, just one man, to understand me. I would like that man to be you." [*Letter to My Judge*]

The reader may easily be disappointed by a given book of Simenon's, expecially when one is already familiar with his method of writing. Surprise and admiration often come with the last pages, which renew, renovate and clarify the preceding chapters retrospectively. One is almost always disillusioned in a detective story by the key to the enigma, since it is much too elementary in relation to the difficulties gratuitously accumulated by the author in the course of his story. Instead of disillusionment and despite all we thought we knew about Simenon, we discover psychological perspectives that we had not anticipated. The watchmaker of Everton needed to have proof of the crime committed by his child in order to realize that Ben and he were, in fact, a single entity. He would let him know of it little by little. It was a secret that he had learned from his father, that he would transmit to his son, and that would go down to his son's son: "Often, in his apartment, in his shop, and even in the street, Dave spoke in a low voice to his father and to the son who accompanied him everywhere. Soon he would speak to his grandson and reveal to him, too, the secret of men." That is how *The Watchmaker of Everton* ends. The very last lines of Georges Simenon's novels almost always have the greatest value: it is there that in a few very simple words, insignificant in appearance, he reveals what he knows about *the secret of men*. A unique secret which manifests itself in a different way according to the individual, but which is summed up to a great extent by the mystery of filiation and paternity once it has been experienced and understood.

The finale of the curious novel *The Time of Anais* is significant in this respect. The conception of persons and things changes back and forth for the reader as well as for the hero. Bauche had decided, even though a little late, to accept the rules of the game. He had admitted, or rather pretended to admit, that he was crazy, since that was what his judges, like the doctor in the *Letter to My Judge,* expected of him in order to explain the inexplicable, to furnish a motive for his crime and to put things back in order again. He had hardly resolved to tell this lie and receive some slight relief (what good is it, in fact, to continue to explain a truth which no one, not even he perhaps, can accept?) when he learns that the only man who had seemed to understand him, the psychiatrist, has actually and without any possibility of appeal, declared him irresponsible:

His eyes opened wide by the strain of suffering for two days and nights, he watched the specialist, whom he now saw for the first time in a white jacket, enter and almost threw himself at his feet in an attitude of prayer:
"I am not really crazy, am I? Not in the way they think?"
Then the psychiatrist, touching him on the shoulder, as if he had the power of laying on hands and curing scrofula, smiled and shook his head.
Bauche had some long years ahead of him in which to explain himself.

These are the last words of the novel *The Time of Anais*. Bauche, who has stopped pretending to be a madman, is, and will be, crazy. But is he really? Was he ever? That no one will know, not even he.

In *Belle*, Spencer Ashby is led little by little to suspect his mental stability. Other people's doubt is contagious. He knows that he is innocent of this particular crime, but reaches the point of wondering whether he wouldn't have been capable of committing it. The same mental process is undergone by Jonas Milk, who, like Spencer Ashby, questions himself as to whether he is sexually abnormal. Certainly he is without great experience, perhaps inhabited by monsters, and, who knows, obsessed? Ashby finally frees himself from his obsession by making his doubts meaningless: since they believe him to be capable of a sadistic crime, since he himself believes it, the only way to settle things with the community and with himself is actually to perpetrate such a murder.

"Admit that you would be annoyed if it was decided that you were irresponsible," Maigret says to a sadistic murderer.

[*Maigret Lays a Trap*] In the same way we see that madness is an explanation which the writer of the *Letter to My Judge* refuses to accept. If they were to take away his sense of responsibility, the idea of his crime would become unbearable to him. He associates himself with his crime only so as to remain faithful to himself. A man must at least know that he is not mad and be aware of the motive for his actions, the indispensable reasons that seem irrational only to those who do not know and do not want to know: judges, juries, and the public at the Court of Assizes. This uncomprehending group includes the psychiatrist in *The Time of Anais* and the addressee of the *Letter to My Judge*. These two novels have much in common, just as *The Little Man from Archangel* has with *Belle*. They are two versions of the same story, as so often happens in Simenon, two essays on the same inexpressible secret.

Even the sexual inspiration in these dramas and in many others is analogous or similar. The large white thighs of Laurette [*Letters to My Judge*] recall the large thighs and affable belly of Anais. We find in *The Fate of the Malous*: "Corine, who was always half naked and who didn't mind showing her large white thighs." In the *Letter to My Judge* Laurette "missed no opportunity to go to bed with a man. She admitted to me that on the days when she expected to have one of those opportunities, she wore no panties, to save time." So did Anais, who "lay in the sun, plump, golden, skirts high, with the thick black triangle of the lower part of her belly well in evidence and there was always a man who would pass by." [*The Time of Anais*] Or take the heroine of *In Case of Emergency*, on the day when she goes to her lawyer's for the first time: "Her glance moved around the room, coming to rest on the only corner of my desk which was not piled up with papers, and then, hiking her skirts up to her waist, she leaned back murmuring: 'You might as well make the most of it before they put me in prison. . . .' She was wearing no pants. It was the first time I saw her slim thighs, her rounded belly of a gamine, the dark triangle of her pubes. . . .''

This is for Simenon a sort of obsession, the origin of which is perhaps to be found in *Pedigree*. The young hero of this book encounters in the alleys of his town "some dirty little girls without pants seated on the edge of the curb, their legs spread wide." Roger is seven when, with a little girl, he invents "a crouching game to see between her legs."

Gina in *The Little Man from Archangel* is recognizable as the young girl, crazy about her own body, who appears in all the latest Simenon books. Provocative, and in wretched poverty, this child awakens the desire and pity of aging men for whom the offer of help will serve as a screen for their enjoyment. If each of these females *pursues the male*, it is because she *does not try to control herself*. The man makes believe he is not jealous, since he fears that he will suffer still more if the one he loves leaves him. Even though *In Case of Emergency* and *The Accomplices*, which immediately preceded it, were much more daring than *The Little Man from Archangel*, we find in this last novel the same connivance between the author and the most debased but also the most desirable of his creatures. A sensuousness loaded with anxiety, poor headstrong love, and a longing for vice as the only possible recourse, lend equivocal beauty to novels that have become more and more serious and confidential. All of them, among other attempts at solving the riddle of man, express a philosophy of physical love. After Kafka and Camus, we are again faced with Georges Bataille. Even Georges Simenon will not allow us to escape this kind of literature. We begin to wonder if it is not the only kind that exists today.

WLADIMIR WEIDLÉ

Les Abeilles d'Aristée (THE BEES OF ARISTAEUS), WHICH Wladimir Weidlé is publishing in a new enlarged version after twenty years, is an important book in that it supplants other works of the same nature. In three hundred and forty-three long and closely spaced pages the author studies the decay of fiction, the disappearance of style, "the reduction of the poem and the picture to the state of a machine designed to produce aesthetic satisfaction," which he ventures to describe as carefully cleansed of all human content. The knowledge which Wladimir Weidlé has of the totality of present-day European literatures, his vast culture in the domain of the arts, and finally his talent as a writer, impel us to view his indictment more seriously than those of the majority of his predecessors.

As usual, his essay on the present fate of arts and letters

combines a pessimistic attitude with an optimistic conclusion. We experience some difficulty in following M. Weidlé in his condemnation of the fictional, poetic, pictorial, architectural, and musical creations of modern times; still more difficulty in sharing his confidence in a forthcoming resurrection, a new art form, which, according to him, will emerge miraculously out of rottenness, like the bees of Aristaeus from tainted entrails. The fact is, we find it very difficult to believe in miracles. To expect salvation from an improbable, from an impossible, marvel, would be still more hopeless for us than for M. Weidlé. He attributes the decadence, indeed the degeneracy, of contemporary art and letters to the loss of a sense of communal spirit, to the lack of any communion. All that remains is to know what communion, what communal spirit, we are talking about. Wladimir Weidlé takes as his point of departure the fact that art has kept a religious content long after all apparent links between the supernatural and the artist have been broken and he concludes that there is no salvation for art except in a return to mystical sources. To survive, or rather to revive, he feels we must find again a mode of thought and creativity associated with this irrational fundamental which is the only reasonable path open to man, so long as he wishes to be in accord with the mysteries of life and its ineffable secret. "The artistic experience, lived integrally, is revealed as rooted in religious experience." This return to the wellsprings postulates a rediscovery of the well-spring of Christianity.

Such a critique implies a continuous reference to the damnation of a civilization deprived of any contact with the supernatural and unaware of the benefits of human and divine communion:

It was not yesterday that a new Moses descended from Sinai, bringing, to replace all laws, only the Multiplication Tables. We have not yet crossed the threshold of the *Age of Enlightenment* when already poetry is slaughtered on the altar of cast iron and concrete where stand in faceless splendor, jealous deities, the four Rules of Arithmetic. . . .

There is nothing here to surprise us, except for the boldness of the imagery. The fault of this work is that we know too often in advance what the author is going to say (if not how he is going to say it, for it is certainly quite impossible to contrive this *poetry slaughtered on a cast-iron altar,* or, elsewhere, these *shackles on the hands of poetry* . . .). Innumerable censors of this century have taken as their theme the dehumanization of man. Most of the censure articulated by Wladimir Weidlé has already been pronounced from the heights of numerous tribunals.

We recognize the buzzing of these happy insects. It was heard all around the scenes of our childhood. I should like to be sure that they are also the bees of the future. "Many around us," writes Weidlé, "have understood that the most direct and sure way to carry art back into breathable air, is by means of a new union of art and religion, of the creative imagination and the Christian faith." But by assuring us that *there are no other paths for the regeneration of art but the one where it encounters the powers of religion,* is he not assuming that the problem of faith is resolved for those who feel and know that they are cut off from the supernatural? These poisons about which Weidlé is severe, are in us, mixed with our mind if not with our soul. The author is particularly hard on mediocre Christians, but he ignores entirely those who never were or are no longer Christian.

The writer of *Les Abeilles d'Aristée* considers that if the miracle of creativity were to cease and if the works of man were to perish from inanition, "it is not because the sacrificer has sinned, it is because he refuses to perform the sacrament. And he refuses because he is no longer capable of shaking off the habit that he has acquired of thinking on every occasion scientifically, technically, statistically. . . ." There are many who do not refuse the sacrament, whatever it may be, but to whom the sacrament is refused. It is not a question of a habit with them, but of their personal mode of thinking, of the only way they still have of believing.

If one does not have faith in the beneficent power of the light with which Wladimir Weidlé softens his criticisms, their presentation loses much of its force. Deprived of their supernatural illumination, his claims change their meaning. From revolutionary in the best sense of the word, which doubtless they appear to men of faith, they become reactionary (but not as in Roger Caillois in an enriching and positive fashion) for those who are only of *good* faith. I speak here in the name of a certain breed of individuals, among whom I belong, whom I call believers without faith. We would like to believe as Saint Augustine would have liked to love. But we cannot. For there exists a group of outcasts forgotten by Wladimir Weidlé: those who, not having chosen their exclusion, would ask nothing better than to re-enter the fold if they could find the gate. Often, in one way or another, they have a presentiment of something sacred, but it always eludes them. They do not say no. They cannot say yes.

For the converter of *Les Abeilles d'Aristée* the creative artist has committed the sin of separating and isolating himself; he has forgotten that the germ of his work in Christian times was *a genuflection and its achievement long prayer*; he has become aware, an unpardonable fault, that he is different:

Once this awareness exists, he will no longer cease to move away from his former working companions; the architect and the sculptor to differentiate themselves from the builder, the mason, the stonecutter; the painter from the calligrapher or the glassmaker; the writer from the scribe (copier or compiler); the composer from the one who gives a sonorous existence to his music. The artist asserts himself and visibly encloses himself in the specifics of his vocation and the irreducible of his personality. Here he is already leaving the community of those who struggle by the sweat of their brow, while waiting to be excluded from the community of those who create, by virtue of the fact that he wants to create according to his law and not theirs. Here he is alone and asks only to be so. . . .

We could multiply quotations of this kind. They reveal in Weidlé the anti-Malraux par excellence. But in this is he not also going against everything that we love in works of art—and against us? For example, the humility that Weidlé demands from the painter does not seem as necessary to us as to him, "Whether or not our painters prohibit themselves from portraying the world," he cries, "the important thing (for them) is that they do not care about it even when they are portraying it and are preoccupied only with their pictures." But isn't it the world that they are trying to catch in the trap of their pictures? In a Cézanne canvas representing some apples, said Malraux, there is certainly more room for Cézanne than there was for Raphael in the portrait of Leon X. He added that Van Gogh's chair impresses us more with the presence of Vincent than with that of a chair. But that does not prove that Raphael is not an irreplaceable artist. Nor is the increased personal touch of Van Gogh or Cézanne in their works a sign of decadence or flight from reality.

Wladimir Weidlé has excellent taste as far as works of art are concerned, even if he is very harsh with regard to the spirit in which they were executed. Theories which seem false to him have nevertheless accounted for works of indisputable quality. His view is that these successes were achieved in spite of the doctrine, and in spite of the artists themselves. An audacious thesis which might perhaps be defensible in certain instances, but which on an arbitrary basis reveals its artificial character. M. Weidlé reproaches Leonardo for having conceived of his pictures more as an engineer than as a painter (this is going pretty far back in his critique of our times, but Leonardo was, it is true, a precursor of them) : "When his genius bursts forth in spite of everything . . . it is because for the moment he must have abandoned the hope of *becoming a kind of god,* and that he himself, on the contrary, was seized by the eternal creative impulse. . . ." We again find this in spite of everything apropos of Dürer whose *"constructed* drawings, born of a passionate study of anatomy and a desire to find at whatever cost a numerical formula for beauty, are striking examples of a victory won by a great genius over his own intentions."

In the same way Zola reached the point, according to Wladimir Weidlé, of creating a few living characters "in spite of all his bad intentions." Tolstoy *obstinately* wanted to match the light of his intellect alone against the darkness of the unconscious but "his genius" saves what he writes in this spirit. Gorki "fortunately did not follow with perfect fidelity" his own literary principles. Proust noted: "In vain did I dine in town, I didn't see the guests because when I thought I was looking at them, I was x-raying them." And Weidlé comments: "Fortunately for his art, it was just the opposite that occurred: however much he might want to be a technician, he could not prevent himself from remaining a poet." As for Valéry, "what he was destined to achieve in poetry, he achieved in spite of himself, against his own will." In fact, "he was a poet only reluctantly." We see how frequently Wladimir Weidlé is obliged to be specious in order to conciliate his pessimistic theories with the most highly acclaimed literature. The latter does not triumph by *defending* itself: it is the attacker, it is Wladimir Weidlé, who defends himself. Caught by an ephemeral scruple, the author of *Les Abeilles d'Aristée* notes: "We should be very unjust and, especially, very ungrateful if we sought to condemn Gide for being what he was." This is, nevertheless, the way he treats most of his authors. But his admiration always takes priority, which he is honest enough not to hide. The least one can say is that this affection for contemporary men of letters clashes somewhat with his steadily advertised contempt for contemporary literature.

The author of *Les Abeilles d'Aristée* marks the limits of his formation, if not of his information, by denying the art of the screen, about which he speaks with surprising scorn. For him "the habitués of the cinema" are all "sheer amusement-lovers"; he puts motion-picture theaters in the same category as restaurants, night clubs, dance halls and "other licensed entertainments." A curious misappreciation of entertainment and the coalescent and at the same time transfiguring effect it has always had on crowds.

Wladimir Weidlé compares the *film-imposture* to the *radio-lie*, without imagining that there can exist any works of art in the cinema. He is right in calling our attention to the fact that the drama of Claudel (of which he speaks admiringly) did not leave its stamp on its period, that it was not implanted there as was that of Sophocles or Shakespeare. "Every collective work contains, besides the element of drama, the element of theater, and the latter is always the fruit of creation that is not individual but collective and is developed, not on the stage alone, but just as truly in the audience. Well, the sources of such creation are dried up in our day." This is not so for anyone who knows the cinema. If Claudel cannot be played on the modern stage, it is because he needs a still more modern one: the screen. M. Weidlé notes that the relative failure of Claudel stage productions does not depend so much "in the last resort on the directors and actors as on the spectators, for the triviality or bombast of the actor is frequently only the reflection of that silent refusal, of that curious secret incredulity, which he senses has penetrated the audience. That the theater was not born with the new drama is not the latter's fault, it is ours." What we need is not a new theater but a new cinema —a cinema that some day, when it discovers Claudel, will reveal him to the multitude. At any rate, the art of the screen exists and it is an art of communion. Such as it is, it has already produced enough masterpieces so that an inventory like that of *Les Abeilles d'Aristée* appears incomplete in treating it so flippantly as not even to take it into account. It would be better, before turning nostalgically to the past, to make full use of the gifts of the present.

Wladimir Weidlé might also be reproached for underestimating his adversaries, and especially the most dangerous of all, the Marxist adversary. The force that Weidlé justly says *never surges forth except from a common religious faith,* is to be found in the U.S.S.R. and among communists throughout the world.

It must be treated seriously. It is true that this communion has not produced the kind of aesthetic results usually associated with this type of collective faith; it has even led to the banning of art, but the reasons for this are too well known for us to dwell on them. For once, M. Weidlé is indeed of his times in so far as he perhaps overestimates art, not its value for man's glory, but its importance for his happiness. In a perfect society there would doubtless be no artistic creation, since no one would feel the need to compensate for any lack. As his equilibrium is unattainable, who would not sacrifice the progress of art for that of man? It is this ever greater amelioration of the state of man that remains as the principal objective. It is what the communists promise and compromise. We reproach them much less for their museums than for their prisons. It all makes sense, and Wladimir Weidlé can write:

In Philistia there is slavery of the artist, but precisely because there is no style. And there is no style because the communal spirit, being obligatory, is without soul and its religion without transcendency, which amounts to saying that, in reality, only a simulacrum of community exists there, supported at great expense by the totalitarian state with the help of a quasi-religion, which, looked at closely, is only a scientific theory in part obsolete, in greater part adulterated, incapable of furnishing art, even in a thousand years, with themes equal to those of the western stained-glass windows of Chartres or of the *Divine Comedy*. . . .

Art again. And art of the past. Dante and Chartres are there. We do not have to look to the future to find them. M. Weidlé does not look as closely as he claims, but from a distance, from far away. To him the U.S.S.R. appears further away from us than the Middle Ages. In a sense he is right, but this should not prevent us from judging the situation as clear-sightedly as possible. The resistance of the Soviet nation to the Nazi invasion did not show "an obligatory and soulless communal spirit." Could a "quasi-religion" have such great apostles and such martyrs all over the world? The real danger lies in the fact that the faith of the Stalin communists is strong enough to eclipse everything that might make them doubt their leaders, if not their cause. The crimes of the Church have not turned many faithful away from its altars. In addition, I doubt whether, in our time, and with the world as it is, the Communion of Saints preached by Wladimir Weidlé would be preferable to the Communion of Men. Even if the latter has been side-tracked, it remains in principle a guarantee of a better-being which is preferable, if one must make a choice, to the better-painting or better-writing desired by the author of *Les Abeilles d'Aristée.*

If we exclude the communist faith, to which we shall return, what does the man of today believe who no longer believes in anything? Jean Rostand will tell us, before we return, with Roger Caillois, Roland Barthes, and a few others to pros and cons of aliterature.

JEAN ROSTAND

IN EXPRESSING *what he believes*, JEAN ROSTAND IS CAREFUL, as usual, not to sound superior. In his concern for exactness, he reverts to certain of his past observations and corrects them, noting for example: "In the almost total ignorance in which we stand as to its starting point and the reasons for its development, it would be unfair to assert—as I myself have had the imprudence to do at times—that evolution occurred in a blind fashion." Or again, in connection with consciousness considered as an epiphenomenon: "After having been won over to the latter point of view, which Le Dantec upheld so vigorously, I have come to feel some doubts in respect to it." He is more precise in *La Vie cette aventure* (Life, the Great Adventure), stating that, raised as he was on the books of Le Dantec and Haeckel, he thought when he was about fifteen that all enigmas were on the point of being solved. Gone are the days of his optimistic youth, when, after reading Lamarck's *Philosophie Zoologique* and Darwin's *Origin of Species*, Jean Rostand saw no real difficulty in the theory of evolution. That "primordial amoebae had raised themselves little by little to the dignity of man seemed perfectly natural to him." Although he has remained resolutely evolutionist, the problem appears less simple to him today:

I have changed a lot since those far-off days. I have put such youthful illusions far behind me, and indeed I must confess that I have acquired a very solid conviction that our ignorance about certain fundamental problems is immense. . . . I am quite convinced that everything in nature is natural, that is to say, I am not tempted to substitute for our admittedly inadequate explanations any metaphysical or mystical solutions which do nothing, in my opinion, but add obscurity to what is already dark enough. But, on the other hand, I am just as much convinced that of this natural order in nature we understand practically nothing.

A profession of faith, or rather of non-faith, which Jean Rostand renews several times in *Ce que je crois* (What I Believe)—which is just as much a *What I Do Not Believe*. But with few exceptions, he is careful not to affirm anything whatsoever, multiplying such prudent formulas as: *I should gladly believe, I should be inclined, I should be tempted at times,* etc. It is the honesty of the savant, which cedes weapons that the believer seizes upon. A Christian will read this upright little book with a feeling of security and perhaps even of superiority. Far from disturbing his own convictions, its rigid soul-searching will only make him feel more sure of them. It appears certain to Jean Rostand that man has sprung, by progressive evolution, from an elementary form of animal life, which appeared on earth about two billion years ago and was the origin of all species. Biology, comparative anatomy, embryology, paleontology, all disciplines confirm what almost all scientists today consider as proved. But we know nothing about the formation of the first living beings; almost nothing about the mechanics of evolution, let alone about the origin of matter, the origin of all things, and the origin of origins. The *credo* which Jean Rostand humbly recites will not fail to reinforce the Christian in his *I believe in God:*

I believe that man comes from an animal, but I have never said that I believed I knew what an animal is. I believe that a child comes—body and mind—from its parents, but I have never said that I believed I knew what giving birth to a child is. I believe that life comes from matter, but I have never said that I believed I knew what matter is.

Religious educators should make the study of this short work obligatory in their schools. A few commentaries are all that would be needed in order to clarify his powerful message. Competent teachers might also usefully include in their program *La Vie cette aventure,* a title that would appeal to young people.

But what will agnostics think of it? Will they be threatened with aggravated metaphysical nausea? It seems not. Jean Rostand is no longer in that state of militant despair and revolt of *Pensées d'un biologiste* (A Biologist's Musings). He seems to have gained and to want to impart a kind of serenity, similar to that of another moralist, Albert Camus, whose *Actuelles II* confirms his earlier attempts in *L'Homme révolté* to surmount nihilism. Jean Rostand, however, is not satisfied with such adventurous solutions. While he, too, offers no other remedy than to make the best of the human malady, he is careful to avoid the shadow of deceit. Risking a bet on "the great and unanswerable questions" is not "a fraudulent wager in the manner of Pascal, in which we are dealt anxiety and infinity," nor is it Camus' offer of "the noonday thought," but rather "a good honest peaceful wager where one can keep all he has." This is what Jean Rostand believes *with his genes, his hormones, his reflexes, his past, his derisive experience, his miserable knowledge . . .*

Jean Rostand does not believe in freedom, since, for him, man's slightest act is strictly determined by heredity and environment. He does not doubt that "two identical germs placed in identical environments will, of necessity, produce two men who act identically." In this he differs from Claude Bernard, for whom determinism, far from being the negation of moral freedom, is its indispensable counterpart. But, Jean Rostand comments in *Hommes de vérité* (Men of Truth), "there is hardly any doubt that by affirming the freedom of the soul, Claude Bernard inflicted a serious blow to his determinist doctrine." This is one of his rare unqualified statements. He believes that if two men were to receive the same hereditary endowment, that if upon leaving the egg they were to undergo the same exterior influences, they would necessarily be identical and indistinguishable in every respect; they would have the same thoughts, the same desires, would act the same way.

Another of Jean Rostand's convictions is that there is no truth to spiritualism: "Upon the inanity of the alleged proofs my conviction extends far beyond the point of believing: I am really sure of being right and it is not my custom to make such clear-cut declarations." On the other hand, "his negation becomes more circumspect in what touches on matters of a metapsychic order." Not that he has the slightest faith in telepathy, second sight, premonition and telekinesis. He does not believe in them, having never, despite numerous attempts, been able to witness a single convincing experiment. But he notes the fact that learned men like Professor Rhine or Julian Huxley, that "eminent psychologists" such as Freud, Laforgue or Merleau Ponty, subscribe to phenomena of this sort. Even though their testimony does not shake his convictions, it does surprise him greatly. In admitting this, "he knows that he is exposing himself to being taxed with stubborn pride, intellectual narrow-mindedness, sectarianism." He has never been present, he repeats, at a single experiment where there did not appear to be, if not fraud, at any rate coincidence, imagination, credulity or a lack of critical spirit. From 1910 to 1911 he frequented the first Society for Psychical Research; later he thoroughly investigated some famous mediums and even the fakir Tahra Bey. Later he frequented the Institute of Metapsychology in Paris, listened to the most reputed seers, experimented with mesmerizers: "So, you see, I have had considerable experience with metapsychology. Well, from it all, I have concluded, without any doubt at all, that there is nothing whatever in it." But even if he admits clearly in *Ce que je crois* that *for him there is more of the inexplicable in protoplasm than in ectoplasm,* we find him on the defensive, an attitude which he never takes with regard to metaphysical beliefs in general or Christianity in particular. Whereas he dismisses religious faith in two words in this little book, he needs close to ten pages (the whole work contains less than a hundred) to deal with spiritism. I am inclined to conclude from this that therein lies his personal nostalgia, his particular temptation, his weak spot, and that if one day (hardly a likely hypothesis) he were to become converted, through lassitude or too great a solitude, it would not be to some religion but some occultism. Besides, what we are dealing with here is, as we noted in connection with Artaud, a vertigo common to many intellectuals today.

Although, in *La Nouvelle Biologie* (The New Biology), Jean Rostand emphasizes the credulity of the great Charles Richet, who went so far as to take the temperature of a phantom, he nevertheless admits in *La Vie cette aventure* that at one time he got hold of a little gadget which, it was claimed, measured "psychic force." As for Charles Richet, he admires his "having had so broad a conception of nature as to include the supernatural," and comments: "Richet has often been criticized for having risked his scientific authority there. What could be more unjust than such a reproach? If, among the piles of nonsense and tricks to which metapsychology seems reduced at present, there were even an atom of truth, that atom would be of such value, and would cause so profound a revision in our intellectual values, that we cannot praise enough those who strive to extract it."

To M. Paul Bodin he says: "I must say that you astonish me when you say that you do not attach much importance to the whole matter! Why, if only a single one of the facts you seem to accept—it is true in a rather offhand sort of way—if only a single one, I repeat, were really to be proved, then I have no hesitation in saying that we should be forced to revise all our conceptions of life and matter. A door would be flung wide open—I do not know onto what prospect, but a door would be flung wide open without any doubt. We should feel less hemmed in, less oppressed by matter. . . ."

Jean Rostand is very concerned about proof, more so perhaps "than in other fields, where he trustfully accepts demonstrations no more satisfactory than these." Here I see another indication that tends to prove what I suggest: he is much too anxious to prove the claims of metapsychology not to be suspicious of them. Here is his admission: "From the time of my youth I have been interested in so-called extrasensory phenomena, and I will even confess that at the outset I was rather inclined to admit their reality." What will happen to him in the event, Jean Rostand does not know, but "he does not consider it entirely impossible that some day the existence of unknown spiritual faculties will be proved."

Coming to what he thinks of the future in *Ce que je crois*, Jean Rostand does not fail to surprise us. He imagines a man still ignorant as to his origin and destiny, but who has "conquered all material obstacles, resolved all social difficulties, navigated among the stars, created matter, perhaps even life, made the species progress by evolving into a superman." I have noted in the margin of the book: "What he believes has become what he hopes." The last words of this work happen to be the very ones that I just used: "But perhaps it is time for me to stop, for I notice that *what I believe* begins to resemble a little too much what I hope...."
The *credo* of our author is that of a man who has faith:

I believe that the democratic idea will triumph without reservations, in the sense that it seems impossible to me that the instincts of justice will not prevail and that the advantage of the many will not outweigh the interest of the few. . . . I am almost sure that the time is no longer distant when one will be amazed to think that throughout so many centuries so much remained the privilege of so few, that society could have been divided into groups that were so unequally treated and that the differentiation was made by virtue of size, intelligence quotients, by resistance to disease, by hope for life, by the marks of criminality.

In another passage, Jean Rostand praises Charles Richet for denouncing a society that, too often negligent of individual merit, grants everything in advance to *the foetus of the rich.* Where we find Jean Rostand optimistic is in his belief in the inevitable triumph of democracy, the democracy that is so sick everywhere in the world, so little able to cope with the problems of modern life. What is not democracy may be infinitely worse, but that is not necessarily a reason for democracy's ultimate victory. "Don't believe that a thing exists just because it would be too horrible if it did not exist; there is no proof by means of the horrible." These lines are from *Pensées d'un biologiste.* Similarly, the passage from *Hommes de vérité* where Rostand suggests that politics, still in an empirical stage, could become an experimental science, seems Utopian. Everything proceeds, however, as though the liberty in which he does not believe actually existed, so that the reactions of the citizens, if not unpredictable, are at any rate unmanageable except by force (propaganda can be considered a technique of violence). Since in the present state of society most individuals are unable to attain a satisfactory development of their physical and intellectual faculties, our society is committing a series of biological crimes: "A day will come, I hope, when the best among men will no longer consider it the supreme reward to see others lacking in what they themselves have in excess." Here again we find Utopia. Of course, says Jean Rostand, it may be necessary to seize by force what should have been granted freely: "But force does not signify violence, especially blind violence—and I believe with Bertrand Russell that things can always be done without violence although they perhaps take a little longer." It is the odd revolt that we know. If one were to amuse oneself in the petty game of comparisons, I would prefer to this Jean Rostand, who reminds us a little too much of Albert Camus, the one in *Pensées d'un biologiste,* who anticipates Jean-Paul Sartre. In 1939 Rostand preceded Sartre's famous: "Man is a useless passion" with "Man is an uninteresting miracle." Less sensitive in tone, the pessimism remains basically unchanged —and total:

Although one is tempted to attribute a higher end to the un-folding of life and thought, one must agree that all of it is passing, transient, fleeting, since one day the earth, like every other planet, must cease to be an inhabitable world, and since, out of the final wreckage, not one of the results of human effort will be saved. No doubt the dead worlds will be replaced by new worlds in which perhaps other cycles of life and thought will be produced, but from one world to another there cannot be any continuity, any transmission, any heritage, each one of them forming a closed system in space and time.

Why this sudden timidity in imagination? Since he is anticipating things, cannot Rostand just as well imagine an interstellar navigator, a new Noah who will take Bach and Van Gogh on board his ark? In answer to this hypothesis, our author replies, in *La Vie cette aventure:* "There can never be any hope of our escaping outside our own solar system, and by the time our little globe is well advanced in its decline, the other planets of our system will not be very desirable places of residence either!" Be that as it may, it has often been noted that Jean Rostand is indifferent to the joys of art, music or painting. The absence of the slightest reference to musical or plastic spheres will strike the reader of *Ce que je crois.* There are a few allusions, on the other hand, to these questions in *La Vie cette aventure* (where he no longer is dealing only with what is most important to him), but they refer only to the origin of genius and not to its results:

All those things in man that are most elevated, rarest, most specifically human, all those things that set him apart from the rest of nature—whether it be the highest example of logical thought or the purest manifestation of feeling—I can see in them only the expansion, the amplification, the exaggeration, of what is already visible in the pullulating and anonymous life of micro-organisms, in the sensitivity of amoebae, in the movements of the plasmodia of myxomycete creeping toward sawdust, in the micro-memory of the paramecia which learn not to ingest harmful dyes.

This passes over in silence what is perhaps a still greater miracle than man's reasoning and feeling: artistic creation. As for the hiatus separating thought from what is not thought, one hesitates to use the tone of the anti-Darwinians after the appearance of *The Origin of Species,* and Jean Rostand himself comments: "What, man with all his genius, with his noble aspirations and urges, the genius of Newton and that of Shakespeare, the categorical imperative of Kant and the quaternions of Hamilton, all of that is supposed to have come from the obscene and hairy animal grimacing in menageries? What an absurd and impudent sacrilege!" And yet these are indeed the words that come to us spontaneously. It is a pretty slim consolation to say with Father Teilhard de Chardin that man *rose* from the monkey. M. Paul Bodin asks Jean Rostand if he ever doubted the scientific explanation concerning the passage from beast to man. He answers: "Never!" In *Ce que je crois* we read:

One of the things that I believe most strongly—one of the rare things of which I am almost sure—is that there exists between us and the animal only a difference of quantity, and not at all of quality; this is because we are of the same stuff, of the same substance, as the animal. This solidarity, this continuity within the animal kingdom—indeed the whole living world—including the human province, must impress anyone who has ever dissected an insect, observed the quivering of a bit of protoplasm, seen an egg shape itself into an embryo. How could I think that anything essential might properly belong only to a single one of the millions of species that people the earth? There is not an organic being, as humble as it may be, to which I do not feel related.

How can we doubt our animal origin when we discover relatively recent vestiges "of animals which were not altogether animals, of men who were not yet altogether men"? As far as the appearance of the first human beings is concerned, Jean Rostand "having no theory to offer, can only admit his ignorance." This does not prevent him from declaring: "I would not like to say that we shall never be able, by artificial means, to raise the apes above their present level, but I feel sure that we shall never be able to make men out of them, no, not even sub-men or pre-men. . . . No [operation] will ever be able to induce in an ape's brain the profound changes of structure which would be absolutely essential for any humanization." Here the believer chalks up his best point.

As for consciousness, properly speaking, I confess that I was ill-informed for a long time. Jean Rostand tells us in *Ce que je crois* in the most categorical way: "Whatever idea one may have in one's mind about the nature of the psyche, it is a biological reality, essential and ubiquitous. Consciousness—the mind, if you wish—is certainly not the appanage of the nerve cells; it exists in a potential or larval state in every cell of every organism: it accompanies all manifestations of life. . . ." He cites Le Dantec speaking freely about the consciousness of atoms; a biologist like Vandel seeing in the organization of matter the first avatar of intelligence; and Julian Huxley, tempted to associate with all matter something that corresponds to a definition of the mind in the higher animals. In consequence the monism of our author does not surprise us, nor his alternate materialism or idealism: "Whether everything be called matter, or everything be called thought, it amounts practically to the same thing."

Although the moralist in Jean Rostand is not absent from *Ce que je crois* and *La Vie cette aventure,* we find no trace of judgments on the behavior of others. No doubt this is because, all in all, he is not sure enough about this kind of evaluation to allow himself to communicate it in such works where he is concerned first of all with himself and secondly with the problems of the species. We again find the moralist in another collection of selected pieces entitled *Pages d'un moraliste.* In it are assembled extracts from the principal non-scientific works of Jean Rostand that appeared from 1920 to 1931: *La Loi des riches* (The Law of the Rich), *Ignace ou l'ecrivain* (Ignatius or the Writer), *Valère ou l'exaspéré* (Valerius or the Exasperated), etc. In rereading these old books, one is struck by the continuity of Jean Rostand's thought; its sharpness has known no slackening, its pessimism no appreciable change, since its earliest expression. It always seems as though savants only give up excessively indulgent moral attitudes to adopt an excessive severity. The bitterness of Jean Rostand is attenuated to the point of being almost unnoticeable. To his interlocutor on the radio who asked him if a certain statement was his final word ("Let's be thankful for life's annoyances, they distract us from its horror"), Jean Rostand answered:

Certainly not. In the first place, that sentence has nothing to do with science. . . . It was the moralist and not the biologist who wrote it. . . . Then it should by no means be taken as a conclusion. . . . Contrary to common opinion, I consider that "thoughts" should express individual and momentary truths. . . . At the moment when life gives us one of those tests of which she is not miserly, suffering overflows beyond the present, and in order to get even with her, one is indeed forced to calumniate life.

Just as the moralist always remains present in the scientific works of Jean Rostand, the experience of the scientist is evident even in his very first books, although he did not combine his literary and scientific activities until 1939, in *Pensées d'un biologiste.* His scientific vocation preceded his talent as an essayist. He was seven years old when he read the first volume of Fabre's *Souvenirs entomologiques,* which "literally transported him," nine, when the famous entomologist offered Mme. Edmond Rostand a sacred scarab for the "fervent neophyte," ten, when Fabre called him "my young disciple," eleven, when Metchnikoff wrote to him: "Your youthful enthusiasm for the sciences makes me predict a fine career as a scientist for you." Since that period he has been, he tells us, "violently evolutionist." His first scientific publication dates from 1920 and his first popular work from 1928. But his scientific works and his meditations about them go back far enough so that Roger Martin du Gard, in *Epilogue,* was able without anachronism to date as of 1918 this note of the dying Antoine Thibaut:

I recollected the exciting conversation that we had in Paris, when Zellinger brought his friend Jean Rostand to spend an evening with us. . . . The situation of Man is extraordinary in this immense universe. It appears to me today with the same clarity as then, when we used to listen to Rostand describe it in his incisive and shrewd voice, with a savant's prudent precision, with a poet's lyrical emotion and freshness of images.

And it is true that he is a poet—and thus he knows that secret universe of beauty from which we had at first imagined him excluded. He is first of all a great writer, with an admirable knowledge of rhetoric, and as such Roger Martin du Gard extols him at the end of *Instruire sur l'homme*. ("A learned man, when he writes well, writes better than anyone," André Maurois remarked in his preface.) We see him capable of transfiguring scientific names and making a kind of incantation out of an enumeration of insects. In a beautiful and little known study on Fabre (included in *Instruire sur l'homme*) we find "the strange Courtilière with its velvety belly, the odoriferous Cicindèle, the heavy Xylocope the color of iodine vapor, the satanic Staphylin with its white caudal horns, the hairless and incarnate larva of Cossus, the sky-blue male of the Hoplie, the alplike Rosalie in pastel shades. . . ." The son of a poet, Jean Rostand has never stopped seeing poetry in nature. Jean Rostand's freshness of soul, his kindness, his desperate and tender love of existence, his faith in man, make him the most brotherly and the most loved of the *men of truth* who are presented in this volume. For what is this literature that is striving so relentlessly to confine itself to what may be proved, if not aliterature?

ROGER CAILLOIS

ROGER CAILLOIS IS ONE OF THE RARE REACTIONARY CRITICS IN contemporary French literature. This amounts to saying that he is one of the only present-day writers with a revolutionary spirit. In fact, in this day in the domain of letters it takes courage, boldness and originality to defend one's posision so continuously, patiently, and still with passionate reasonableness.

There are few authors studied in this series against whom the work of Roger Caillois does not provide some harsh judgments: "More than one [writer] confines himself to mentioning what he has done or wanted to do, what he has thought, felt or dreamed. No need to go to any trouble. The less the notes are polished, the more value is attached to them. The roughest are considered the best; this rubbish is priced according to volume. The only merit required of these disparate and trivial confidences is that they hide

nothing, and above all that they blurt out what is ordinarily
kept quiet: the immoderate and ignoble, the sordid and in-
famous, the ridiculous and burlesque. A promotion of waste
products." [*Babel*] Thus Roger Caillois, an exemplary
alittérateur himself, accuses aliterature of complacency:
"These are nothing but heartrending confessions, cries of
alarm and despair, blasphemies and nightmares, messages,
digressions or prophecies. . . ." Since he is antiromantic, he
is *a fortiori* antisurrealist. One of his essays, *Les Impostures
de la poésie* (The Tricks of Poetry), demonstrates the inanity of the pretensions of those who want the poet to be
"a wizard or a prophet, a *seer* or a metaphysician."

The excesses of literary freedom constantly preoccupy
Caillois. "In the city," he writes in the beginning of his
Vocabulaire esthétique, "there are few things that one must
hold so dear as freedom. But in Letters, where everything
is freedom from the outset—I mean where the city does not
intervene, where no constraint is obligatory—to do as one
pleases is only laziness, a lack of audacity and ambition. It
is to content oneself with nature. Art demands more." The
words most often used by the author of *Babel* and *Les
Impostures de la poésie* are *discipline, effort, conquest.*

"Civilization is nothing but a continuous conquest by man
of himself." [*Le Rocher de Sisyphe* (The Rock of Sisiphus)]
In *Babel*, however, he ridicules this sort of statement.
(" 'Justice,' " he begins, 'is nothing but a decision to . . .'
That's enough. I already know that justice admits of other
interpretations . . . .") He is professing one of the truths
closest to his heart. "With words and formulas you can
speak and write as much as you want. You need neither experience nor reflection. Why deprive oneself? There are
those who cannot express themselves differently." Caillois

is dealing with something he knows well. The devices of language, whenever he gives in and uses them, help him to find fault with these devices themselves.

To accept no restraint is to deprive oneself *of the faculties which serve to construct and dominate.* [*Les Impostures de la poésie*] "Hence modern literature: its disdain for style, its rejection of all rules, and the almost exclusive predominance of those genres that are best suited to license in thought and writing, where one sees, not without candor, the sign of sincerity and inspiration." [*Babel*]

In *L'Incertitude qui Vient des rêves* (The Doubt That Comes from Dreams), Roger Caillois takes care to recall the durability of his preoccupations and the continuity of his research: "I mean an uninterrupted attraction for the force of instinct and vertigo, the desire to define them, to take away as much as possible from their sorcery, to understand their powers, in short, to pit against them the pre-eminence of intelligence and will, because only these faculties give man a chance to be free and creative." He refers, not only to the aforementioned works on poetic inspiration, but to his studies devoted to the syntax of the sacred, the vertigo of war, or the exigencies that produce games.

The forces he calls in turn instinct, vertigo, intoxication, ecstasy, delirium, frenzy, the abyss, exercise a fascination on him. Even though he suspects that he probably has a subconscious feeling of *connivance* with these automatic reactions, he states, while discussing dreams, that in spite of this he is unwilling to surrender to them:

While I refused to be duped by their illusions, I undertook at least to clarify their mystery, without seeking to depreciate their qualities. I wanted to evaluate them in their excellence, measure them at the height of their power. I tried to pierce the obscurity of the inaccessible laboratories where elementary and decisive fermentations develop in the sleep of the conscious. Sometimes I recognized in them virtues and properties about which their most enthusiastic prophets had remained silent. As much as it was in my power, I high-lighted these neglected assets. I made it a point of honor to give them every advantage.

It is the greatness of the mind, Roger Caillois confesses in *Les Impostures de la poésie*, that it is always tempted to surrender to seductions of this kind: "To win divine rewards at least it should be aware every moment, with all the more acuteness the more elevated it is, of the calls that invite it to fall and offer it easy treasures. It is necessary for it to hear them but not to respond. From the never-ending struggle, from this delayed victory, come the power and the honor which a quick and simple victory would not yield." This kind of disguised and secret confession is frequent in a very modest author who avoids the personal note as much as possible. (Cf. the appendix to *Le Rocher de Sisyphe*.) They none the less remain, hidden and touching, like a filigree in his writing: "If this is the place for a confidential note, I have always felt more disposed to fight poetry than to abandon myself to it. . . ." [*Les Impostures . . .*] A confidence, completely intellectual like the others, but with moral overtones that are evident. In *L'Incertitude qui vient des rêves*, there is another confession whose purpose makes it more concrete. In order to talk about dreams, Roger Caillois cannot do other than to evoke his own dreams. Refusing traditional clues as well as psychoanalytic explanations, he does not realize that he runs the risk of betraying himself by describing his dreams. They afford a twofold source of interest: that which is found in them by the author (for whom, we shall see, the very fact of dreaming is more worthy of examination than the material of which these dreams are made), and the other, unknown or neglected by him, which allows us to plunge briefly into the very depths of a life whose secrets it holds. We belong indeed to the race he complains of: that of the reader who is more interested in the writer than in what he writes.

When he studies a poet, Roger Caillois does not fall into this temptation so common today. Here again he "frankly takes the opposite position." When, for example, he examines the work of St.-John Perse, "he is not interested in the author, nor his torments, nor in his secrets, nor even in his readings. He acts practically as if the author did not exist.":

After all, criticism consists of studying the technique and significance of a work, much less the biography and psychology of a man. This is vain curiosity or a matter for psychoanalysis, if one concedes that psychoanalysis is anything other than a conjectural science where a docile principle of explanation offers far less resistance to the interpreter than, for example, stars offer to the astrologer.

Roger Caillois, by saying too little about himself in connection with his dreams, avoids confessing what he does not want to make known.

His *Poétique de St-John Perse* proves "that it is possible to speak of poetry without mystery and without metaphysics." Avoiding what may be vague, he reminds us that poetry, freed from illusion, is first of all *treatment of language*. That explains his meticulous study, sentence for sentence, word for word, sometimes letter for letter. While he refuses to succumb to the vertigo of the abyss, or even to lean over that attractive void, he is not unaware of its appeal. One of his most frequent comparisons (it is found in almost every one of his books) is that of the flower, masterpiece of nature which the masterpieces of man cannot imitate. He is aware that, taken apart petal by petal, the poetry of St.-John Perse remains an inimitable flower. The same holds true for every dream, but this should not preclude its methodical analysis: "botany is possible and worthwhile."

In discussing the *difficulties that arise from the simple fact of dreaming*, Caillois once more goes against the tide. On questions of art for art's sake and of literature, on the definition and use of the poetic image, on the nature of inspiration, "he had to convince himself that he had ideas which were as opposed as one could imagine to those that were generally in favor." [*Vocabulaire esthétique*] Similarly, as against dreams he opposes "one of the most noble oddities of the human mind, which is to strive stubbornly to find a meaning in what has none, and thus to draw some significance out of the insignificant." While he considers dreams "a sham disorder without secrets," he realizes that this is not a comfortable attitude, even for him:

It is not always easy, for dreams have a thousand tricks to make one believe that they are, in fact, bringing a mysterious message, and that all that is needed is to take the trouble to decipher it. The best protected mind and the one most determined to avoid this foolishness succeeds indeed nine times in succession, but is still naïve enough to succumb the tenth time. I think what is almost irresistible to man is the temptation to lend a meaning to everything which, at one and the same time, seems capable of having one and yet indefinitely resists interpretation.

Even in his careful and lucid essay, *L'Incertitude qui vient des rêves*, Roger Caillois allows this half-confidence to slip through with his customary honesty and discretion: "Perhaps also my effort only signifies that, in spite of myself, without realizing it, with more shame, trickery and evasions than is my custom, I belong to the large group of those who use sleep as a refuge, dreams for happiness."

To the extent, which is not small, to which Caillois escapes magic spells, he reveals once more his militant antisurrealism. It is from dreams, or from madness, he states in *Les Impostures*, that certain poets, modern "heirs of Pythia," seek their inspiration. Once more he evokes the fallacious paradise of dreams, a promised land that one reaches only to find it spurious. He ridicules the recent disciples of the German Romantics who take notes on and publish their unembellished dreams in order to capture thereby a flow of poetry. In contrast to the surrealists, it is the coherence of dreams that strikes Caillois. He does not believe that the absurd or fantastic can be the principal component of dreams. On the contrary, they too are substitued for reality only to make us aware of necessity. They are just as precise as if they existed in the waking state. Some chains of events seem logical to us until we are no longer asleep, and then their unreasonableness strikes us. But up to then, they convince us. One of the principal themes of this essay is that dreams give an impression of all the workings of the mind, even the most complicated: "I am sure of it: there is no operation of the intelligent, active, and responsible consciousness of which the dream cannot furnish the counterfeit in the passive, mechanical, and spellbound mode. More than one dream has furnished me with proof of this."

The surrealist predilection for enjoying and remembering only the incoherence in dreams is, therefore, according to Roger Caillois—who proves with examples what he affirms —"the method which is least capable of communicating the illusion of the dream and of reproducing its power artificially." Hence the error of the editors of the *Révolution surréaliste* in the special section of that review devoted to dreams, where they stress the marvelous without taking into account the fact that "the inconsistencies, the contradictions, the impossibilities, never appear as such to the dreamer, who accepts them as natural":

As their doctrine impels them, on the one hand, to identify the dream and the wildest fantasy, and on the other, to oppose the dream with logic and reality as much as possible, their accounts are certainly likely to be disconcerting, but they do not at all give the impression of being dreams, precisely because they purposely cast aside verisimilitude while at the same time they take care to emphasize it by means of all kinds of appropriate adjectives. This is working in the wrong direction, for the dream gives one, in relation to itself, an irrefutable impression of evidence and reality.

Roger Caillois cites the opposite example of Kafka, who, by accumulating in his novels the small precise facts, the incontestable features taken from life, gives an agonizing impression of truth to a reality that is, nevertheless, indubitably of the dream world. "In *The Trial* or in *The Castle* the descriptions are as detailed as possible and almost tiresome." Kafka is one of the only ones, according to Caillois, who not only resolves the *literary* problem of the dream but also clarifies it with real understanding. In his admiration for Kafka, Roger Caillois again shows where he is different. We prefer this reasonable approbation, given lucidly to a lucid writer, to so much stuttering adulation. The author of *Metamorphosis* is, in fact, most often praised, not for his clairvoyance, but for that part in the shadow, where *planned* literary activity permits him at least to make witchcraft more tolerable, if not to exorcise it.

The writer who glorifies the freedom of the artist most effectively is not André Breton (to the relative extent to which he writes according to his principles), it is Roger Caillois. We read in *L'Incertitude qui vient des rêves:* "Freedom only exists where intelligence and courage succeed in nibbling away at fate." It is this sense of fatality, in its various aspects, that he has fought in his entire work and that he attacks again here. Studying the dreams of man and comparing them with what he sees once he is awake, Roger Caillois cannot but come across the problem, one of the oldest in philosophy, of the distinction between dream and reality. While he does not neglect its theoretical character, which he often stresses, he does not think that he can offer any reassuring solution, as Descartes finally did. To his way of thinking, reflection on dreams "leads to an ultimate conviction that no amount of reasoning can shake": *there is no infallible criterion that allows anyone, at whatever moment, to be absolutely certain that he is not actually in the process of dreaming.* But in spite of the thoroughness and patience of his exposition, the purely speculative character of Roger Caillois's latest essay makes it less interesting. On the other hand, his views on the profound coherence of dreams are invaluable. They form part of a broader undertaking, begun a long time ago and continued through the years. From the outset he has taken the same reasonable stand that appears bold only because of the unjustifiable discredit into which such concepts have fallen.

ROLAND
BARTHES

ALTHOUGH *Le Degré zéro de l'écriture* (ZERO DEGREE OF Writing) is presented by its author, Roland Barthes, as a working hypothesis, it has a dogmatic tone.

The clarity that classical writing requires is by no means an obligatory quality of language for Roland Barthes. "That is because the pre-bourgeoisie of monarchical times and the bourgeoisie of post-revolutionary times, using the same form of writing, developed an essentialist mythology of man, classical writing, one and universal, abandoned all deviation in favor of a continuum of which each particle was a *choice,* that is, a radical elimination of all that is possible in language. Political authority, dogmatism of the mind and the unity of classical language are, therefore, figureheads of one and the same historical movement." By seeking to disjoint and disintegrate language so that the mechanism of its subterfuges comes apart and the possible falseness is exploded, the most subtle representatives of aliterature are led to neglect the primary purpose of words and their *raison d'être,* which is to signify something.

Making a choice between possibilities, avoiding the indistinct in word and writing in order to make the expression as exact and specific as it can be, that precisely is the object of spoken and written language. Classic clarity becomes for Roland Barthes "the ideal appendix of a certain discourse, that very discourse whose abiding objective is persuasion." Thus, what is the heart and body of language changes into a superfluous organ. Roland Barthes, who writes with limpidity, has not deprived himself of this appendix. No writer could ever do so as long as he wanted to make himself understood. It would be an operation whose dangers have already been shown by experiment.

According to Roland Barthes, "writing is in no way a means of communication." As the opposite of spoken language, it is by nature a *counter-communication.* Its particular ambiguity is in that it is *at the same time language and coercion.* Since all paradoxes, however laden with truth they may be, are capable of being turned around, one could say just as correctly that it is speech that aims to remove adherence by intimidating means, and one attribute to writing the opposite character of a balanced, delicately shaded, essentially *honest* act. To the extent to which "it improperly combines the reality of acts to the ideality of ends" political writing is, however, by all evidence, coercive. Roland Barthes devotes a chapter to it which is all the more convincing in that his arguments appear to be political. Literary writing also fulfills the author's definition if we agree with him that since it is an instrument placed in the service of a class ideology it imposes its myths more than it proposes them. One can obviously play upon the word communication. But whether or not, in either case, it is a one-way transmission, changes nothing in the fundamental purpose of language, which is to make oneself understood. This elementary truth Roland Barthes knows as well as anyone else. He is right in not being satisfied with it, but wrong in forgetting it on the way.

Roland Barthes is on Rimbaud's side. So are we. But we can still be on Chénier's (for example). Roland Barthes and his kind dispense with what is contrary to their beliefs a little too easily. (There is something religious in their dedication to Rimbaud and his breed.) It would surprise me if all poets before Rimbaud were as unrealistic as we are assured they were. I imagine Chénier sometimes wrote poetry in the sense understood by Roland Barthes. So did Ronsard, Racine, and many others who are as great poets as Nerval, but less mad. What remains to be understood is whether they really did not know what they were doing when they stopped considering poetry (Roland Barthes dixit) as "prose decorated with ornaments or amputated of its liberties" and risked the great poetic adventure, thanks to the richness of words and the results of their chance encounters.

Roland Barthes is right in indicating that modern poetry opposes classic art with a difference that affects the whole structure of language. The fact that we have retrospectively discovered some elements of modern art in classical poetry should disturb his conscience, not as a political, but as a poetic revolutionary. In the heart of classical language, even poetic language, no word is *dense* of itself. It is less a symbol than a path of linkage. Tradition accordingly absorbs the freshness of words and forces one to avoid "the sonorous and semantic accident which concentrates the savor of language on one point and halts its intellectual development in favor of a poorly distributed sensual pleasure." For Roland Barthes modern poetry is quite different. It starts not with Baudelaire but with Rimbaud:

Beneath each word of modern poetry lies a sort of existential geology, in which is assembled the total content of the Name, and no longer its selective content as in classical prose or poetry. The word is no longer directed in advance by the general intent of socialized speech: the consumer of poetry, deprived of the guidance of selective associations, comes upon the Word head-on, and receives it as an absolute quantity, accompanied by all its possibilities. . . . This Hunger for the word, common to all modern Poetry, makes the poetic word a terrible and inhuman word. It establishes a speech full of holes and full of lights, full of absences and of super-nutritive signs, without prevision or permanence of intent, and thereby so opposite to the social function of language that the simple recourse to a discontinued word opens the way to all Supernatures.

In short, in modern poetry "the thought" is "prepared, installed, little by little, by the chance of words." Roland Barthes put *thought* in quotation marks to show that it is not thought in the classical sense. What other connotation than the classical one could this word have? "The social function of language" is appealed to in order to make us understand that we are in a basic domain, more arcane than that of the relations between social groups. But this "socialized speech" has no relevance here: we are only dealing with the inner dialogue, from oneself to oneself, where a thought is born and develops.

Naturally, this does not constitute a case against the value of modern poetry. Dialectics and poetry are two different things. I simply want to say that I do not feel compelled to consider all poetry that is not labeled modern uninteresting just because its own form of modernness does not have the desired sense. Baudelaire's poetry, for example, combines the fluorescence and phosphorescence dear to Barthes with the advantages of a coherence that he distrusts. "Modern poetry is an objective poetry. There nature becomes a discontinuum of solitary and terrible objects." So solitary that each one who reads finds what he wants, as well as he can. Therefore it is difficult, almost impossible, to judge it and hence the absence, to date, of all criticism. The last real criticism of contemporary French poetry dates from the Occupation, when the political situation helped us to understand poetry. How are we to recognize it now when language has been purposely befogged?

When Roland Barthes cannot avoid mentioning a modern poet, "one of those who follow through on their plan and consider Poetry not as a mental exercise, a state of soul, or the taking of a position, but as the splendor and freshness of dreamed language," whom does he find to cite? René Char, obviously. René Char is always mentioned and only he, because he has received official recognition from the critics. Here is the desert to which his words lead, the words whose inhuman character is admired, "the speech full of terror which brings man into contact not with other men but with the most inhuman images of nature: heaven, hell, the sacred, childhood, madness, pure matter, etc." What is surprising, once more, is not that such poetry is liked and defended, but that a clean sweep is deliberately and remorselessly made of everything else. I, too, am a fervent (if not completely accredited) admirer of René Char. That doesn't prevent me from liking Jules Supervielle, for example.

We end up with, in Roland Barthes' own words, "a silence of writing." This *subversive scuttling of Literature, this art which has the very structure of suicide* (from Rimbaud's silence to Mallarmé's typographical agraphia) brings us "to the doors of a world without literature about which, however, it will be up to the writers to testify." There is another solution, less spectacular but no less exemplary, according to our author: blank writing or *zero degree of writing.* This neutral style is no longer "a formal instrument placed in the service of a triumphant ideology," but "a silence's way of existing," a sort of pure equation "having no more obscurity than an algebraic symbol before man's depths." "It is indisputably a victory for Sartre that they never said that he wrote well. . . ." Although this remarkable sentence (from an article by Roland Barthes published in *Combat* in 1947 and also called *"Le Degré Zéro d'écriture"*) was dropped from the essay of the same name, it none the less sums up his position. Similarly, our author admired Camus for having obtained in *L'Etranger* "a style of absence which is almost an ideal absence of style." The piece in *Combat* pointed out that it was concerned with *this philosopher's stone of the writers of today,* and added: "Can a writer of Camus's breed escape the flaubertization of writing? There is the tragic dimension of the dilemma." Writing, henceforth, should be invisible, so that the writer may find his innocence again. Does this mean, then, that he feels guilty? Roland Barthes explains:

The ideological unity of the bourgeoisie produced a single type of writing; in bourgeois times (that is, the classical and romantic eras), form could not be rent asunder, since consciousness was not; on the contrary, from the moment when the writer ceased to be a witness to the universal and became an unhappy consciousness (about 1850), his first act was to choose a form, by either accepting or rejecting the writing of the past. Classical writing, therefore, exploded, and the whole of literature, from Flaubert to our days, has become a problem of language.

In other words, there is little difference between the writing of a Fénelon and a Mérimée, of a Laclos and a Stendhal, since the bourgeoisie, having control of intellectual power well before the Revolution, kept it intact until 1848. Writing, then, is an excellently prepared instrument which professionals employ without asking themselves any questions about it. It is class-writing placed in the service of class-politics:

The unity of classical writing, homogeneous for centuries, the plurality of modern writings, multiplied for the last hundred years to the very limit of literary possibility, this kind of explosion of French writing corresponds to a great crisis in all History, apparent in a much more confused manner in literary History proper. What separates the "thought" of a Balzac from that of a Flaubert is a variation of school; what opposes their writings is an essential rupture, at the very moment when two economic structures form a juncture, bringing into their articulation decisive changes of mentality and conception.

In place of a refusal to write, Roland Barthes sees no better solution than the zero degree of writing. Thanks to this blank writing, "the human problem is disclosed and delivered without bias, and the writer is always an honest man." Before Camus, he was honest only at the price of silence or involuntary chance events. This, for example, was true of Proust, one of the few great French writers spared by Roland Barthes, because in him "literature is no longer a pride or a refuge, it becomes a lucid act of [imparting] information, . . . it assigns to itself the duty of rendering an immediate account, preliminary to any other message, of the position of men walled in by the language of their class, of their region, of their profession, heredity or history."

It is instructive to refer here to Dionys Mascolo's essay, *Le Communisme*, which we shall discuss in the next chapter. This author also suspects most of our great writers living or dead of bad faith, and condemns all but a few who more or less correspond to those whom Roland Barthes has gathered into his ark and snatched away from the flood. Among them is Proust. But, according to Dionys Mascolo, the phenomenology of Proust was not intentional. "He did not know that he was putting the universe in parentheses in order to see and describe his object better. . . . These characters, this society, seem miraculously involuntary; this is because the objective of the author was not to describe them. He did not want that, he never wanted anything but to describe the effect that time has on a separate experience." We recognize this characteristic of the terrorist school of Barthes's and Mascolo's type: a tendency, in order to prove their point, always to increase as much as possible the part played by chance, to make the authors, if not unaware, at any rate less aware than they actually are. These literary revolutionaries (whether it be this red terror or the white terror of Wladimir Weidlé) only snatch their victims from oblivion to place them in some sort of limbo.

Roland Barthes recognizes, it is true, Marcel Proust's *lucidity* in imparting information. But how many other authors whom we consider important chiefly because of the authenticity of their testimony, are downgraded by him! He dismisses the writing of a craftsman whose principal value stems from the labor that it has entailed. The author of *Degré zéro de l'écriture* mentions, not without disdain, "Gautier (impeccable master of Belles-Lettres), Flaubert (prowling among his phrases at Croisset), Valéry (in his room early in the morning), or Gide (standing before his desk as if before a workbench) . . ." Gide, he said, preferred "the security of art to the solitude of style":

Workmanlike writing, located in the interior of the bourgeois heritage, does not disturb any order: deprived of other struggles, the writer possesses a passion which suffices to justify him: giving birth to form. Even if he renounces the liberation of a new literary language, he can at least improve on the old, load it with intentions, preciosity, splendors, archaisms, create a rich and fatal language. This great traditional writing, that of Gide, Valéry, Montherlant, even Breton, signifies that form, in its weightiness, its extraordinary trappings, has a value that transcends History, as, perhaps, the ritual language of priests.

That Gide, Valéry, Montherlant, and Breton may prefer, to the liberation of language, the liberation of whatever within them aspires toward elucidation and can be expressed only through the medium of whatever style they deem best suited to their purposes, does not enter Roland Barthes' mind. This is too easy; its very simplicity eludes him. The new school of criticism only feels at home in subtlety. But there is no greater blindness than that of the overstimulated intelligence that wants to dig where there is no depth. One can say of these literary revolutionists that they are terrorized terrorists, talking out loud in their personal darkness, giving themselves airs of flippancy. In fact, lacking confidence, full of inferiority complexes, they try to eliminate values for which they no longer have any use, breaking the instruments which their predecessors employed so brilliantly and seeking a field where competition is no longer possible. The domain they have selected is criticism, even when they are themselves engaged in creative work. From zero degree of writing we have come to the freezing point of criticism: that which fixes a previously deformed reality and immobilizes it in its caricature. Or else it is the nth degree of this same criticism, where thought, heated to the maximum, burns whatever it touches and causes it to float off in smoke.

I, too, admire Blanchot, Cayrol, Queneau, and Sartre, whom Roland Barthes considers, along with Camus, as almost the only living writers worthy of interest. But their current prestige does not give me the right to plunge their predecessors into the shade. In my opinion, Gide, Valéry and Breton do not write *too* well, first of all, because no one ever writes too well (or else they would write badly). Furthermore (may it not displease Roland Barthes and his friends), this writing is suited to its objective, which is to express something, and what Gide, Valéry and Breton expressed seems to me as important, perhaps more important, than what certain of Roland Barthes's masters say in their terrible blank voices. Aliterature is evident also in Breton, and especially Valéry. And look at the *literature* that is evidenced by Camus!

DIONYS MASCOLO

IN HIS WORK *Le Communisme,* WHICH BEARS THE SUBTITLE: *Révolution et communication ou la dialectique des valeurs et besoins* (Revolution and Communication, or the Dialectic of Values and Needs), Dionys Mascolo studies in particular *Communism and the role of the writer.* This piece is interesting for its truth as well as its falsehoods, for its intelligence as well as its stupidity, for its faith as well as its bad faith. Moreover, it is a good tonic and, in short, *sympathique.*

The unpardonable and scarcely avoidable weakness of literature is, for Mascolo, its simplification: *The fact of simplifying breaks communication. The simplest man is less simple than the simplified image of him. Nothing is so irritating as to see presented and accepted as true the simplified image of one's own life.* This is true and painfully felt by numerous writers: those who through weakness have placed themselves in a defensive position or who were placed there through the weakness of their friends. This attitude is never true of the Communists. Mascolo seems to think only of attack. He leads it bravely and even with drums beating; the furor and noise are necessary so that the combatant shall not ask useless questions, especially the most dangerous of all: Am I in the right, have I examined my adversary's cause? Although fighting on the sidelines of the great Communist struggle, which gives him the freedom to maneuver, Mascolo behaves none the less like a relatively disciplined guerrilla. Of course, he permits himself to make allusions (as we shall point out) to what orthodox Communists arbitrarily pass over in silence. That gives his discourse, sometimes unusually personal, the tone of confession. But as for what is essential, the Communist struggle for Communist victory, he is as good a warrior as anybody. If he sometimes seeks to avoid the simplification for which he reproaches his enemies, he does not do it continuously. Either his good faith is not proportionate to his faith, or his intelligence has some curious failings.

"I only want to indicate that in the final analysis the only defensible simplification is materialistic simplification. . . ." This "in the final analysis" is a sign that there is something heretical in Mascolo's Communism. It is a sign of relative Communist weakness, therefore of relative moral strength in the traditional sense of the term. But it is only a half-admission, which he wants people to forget immediately. By little correctives of this sort, Mascolo believes he has satisfied his conscience and the conscience of others. Only the tone of the assertion following that of the interrogation gives us the clue. We remember the postulate: the only defensible simplification is the Communist simplification. We shall not forget it, first, because we shall find it constantly professed in the same peremptory fashion; and, next, because the author, passing on to the application, will practice what he preaches.

Dionys Mascolo questions all the works of man, from the time that men have existed, men who have tried to understand something about what they are and what they do. The only concepts that escape his revision are the fundamentals of Communism or those of the Communist as he actually is. It is possible that a few of his personal discoveries will one day become gospel for the Communists, who will discreetly pass over in silence the excommunication to which this father of the Church was subjected. While he has borrowed much from the right and from the left (especially from the left, of course), he is the first to express certain truths with convincing persistence. I find fault with them only in that they require the destruction or at least the denial of more ancient truths, whose scope is just as broad in a different way. For Mascolo, as for every believer, there is only one truth. In his youth when he was *at the height of his relativist naïveté* he used to think: to each his own truth. We shall have occasion to point out anew that, according to him, the truth of Communism is that *there is no truth*. At any rate, it is a question of a truth that Mascolo considers exclusive. Hence his manner of treating his adversaries in cavalier fashion; hence his voice which judges, excommunicates, condemns. The Communist universe is Manichaean. This is something—let us repeat once more after Malraux— that cannot be accepted by individuals who are called intellectual, who are always afraid of not paying sufficient attention to nuances. I know that this species may seem to be on their way to extinction. The temptation of Communism acts more and more on intellectuals because they are tired, in the long run, not of trying to understand, but of feeling themselves alone in an act of comprehension that must be started over and over again. I don't mean alone as a body, I mean individually (hopelessly) alone. And faith is a refuge, especially a faith shared by an immense number of men and women the world over, who are precisely the men and women from whom one does not want to be separated, even though one is responsible for the separation. They have no opportunity to speak and of all the miseries of the proletariat this is the least pardonable. On this point as on numerous others, I am in agreement with Mascolo: "The existence of an anonymous human group, of a vast human *element* as impersonal as water or air and as mute," is inadmissible to the extent to which "it makes one incapable of conceiving the possession of the simplest truth other than as a privilege." These qualms of conscience are the great intellectual development of modern times. It goes back a little more than a hundred years. That is, it is as old as Marxism. Let us give the floor to Dionys Mascolo. This is not the only time our ideas will coincide:

At the moment that this is being written, one knows—I know, you know, everybody knows—that a million Hindus are to die, will die, of starvation within the year. All right: it is not death that is so distressing. Man is mortal, and the some two billion now alive will all be dead before long. The irritating thing is that since all this exists and is known—that a million Hindus will die within the year—there is no truth possible. It means that no communication, no expression, is possible. . . . I cannot speak [to the Hindu who knows he is going to die]. He cannot hear me. No one can say anything to him. There is someone whom you can't convince, to whom you can't even think of *talking. Consequently, it is he who is right.* This amounts to saying, either that it is not possible to speak or that one should arrange things so that what is said is acceptable to the one who is about to die of starvation in this world where the primary occupation of some is to speak, to say things. It is not a political consideration that makes one concern himself with India, with families, with socialism, with revolutions. It is the need to assure communication. It is universal or it is nothing.

It is too true that we are *private possessors of the means of expression.* The pangs of conscience which result from this are, we have seen, the source of a fundamental modification of literature called by Roland Barthes the *zero degree of writing.* Writers "face to face with the harsh disparity of modern society" have discovered their responsibility, or, more exactly, the responsibility of literary language, "a fate which encloses us and labels us, and separates us from other men." For about a century, writing was expected to be something different from an instrument in the service of a class ideology. It was expected to be communication, communication that includes man but goes beyond him, and it is in modern poetry, Roland Barthes tells us, that words have the terrible weight of things. Communication with men taken in their totality, and it is the central theme of Dionys Mascolo's book. He declares that if henceforth there is to be only one general problem, Communism, it does not help at all to be right in some details: "The works of non-Communism, whatever they may be, never allow one to recover anything but properties and faculties piecemeal. And piecemeal properties and faculties are of little value when they can only be acquired in the height of misfortune or delirium." The result is a thorough condemnation of everyone, not only of those who oppose his postulate, but even of those who do not recognize its absolute value, in theory as well as in practice.

The postulate is offered from the very first line of Mascolo's essay: "We must understand from the outset that the only question really necessary from now on is that of Communism. This should be a self-evident truth, since ordinarily just to express it is enough to obtain the assent of all." The author disguises his statement with ostensible reservations to make it appear less dictatorial. But here is something even more precise: "Every search for truth, every occupation, way of life, attitude, or plan . . . *pursued apart from the Communist undertaking, has lost all significance*. Or else it only retains a significance so humble, so limited, that it would not occur to anyone to speak about search for truth in connection with it." The party spirit clearly turns to arbitrary blindness here (we shall come back to this unintelligence peculiar to a certain form of militant intelligence): it ends in obvious untruths. It is hardly necessary to say that no one should speak in a tone of certainty about such unjustifiable generalizations.

Dionys Mascolo's writing is coercive; it menaces, it intimidates; in brief, it is counter-communication. All these expressions are applied by Roland Barthes in *Le Degré Zéro de l'écriture* to writing in the broadest sense, although they seem particularly apt in relation to political writing. It is regrettable that there may be applied to Mascolo, the apostle of communication, not only these expressions but another statement by the same author: "In the present state of History, all political writing, offered as description and judgment at the same time, can only confirm the existence of a police universe." Mascolo himself admits: "To take the floor and speak may only be a certain kind of violence.

It is like taking power. Speech is a certain power. . . ."
To be more specific, so that his own statements will not be
turned against him: "The act of taking the floor escapes
being violence only if there is . . . a need for communication."
He means: if it is a Communist who speaks (or writes) as a
Communist. Violence ceases to be violence if it is a question
of Communist violence. None the less, it loses not the least
of its attributes. We are familiar with this Communist subversion of language: where *peace* signifies *war* and *liberty,
slavery*. It is found in every political speech, in all political
writing, but to a lesser degree in the other parties, which at
least try to keep up appearances. It is the strength of the
Communists that they need no longer have recourse to
hypocrisy, not even to the hypocrisy of language. This signifies an absence of remorse, that is, a feeling of non-guilt
and even of innocence. Lucky men.

If for Mascolo evil comes from simplification, what simplification are we concerned with, or rather are we not to be
concerned with? "All incomplete truth," he writes, "and
all of it is necessarily incomplete. Therefore, all truth which
is not presented as being incomplete constitutes a falsehood."
In the name of what exception that would prove the rule
does our author exclude himself and Communism from this
censure? He judges his own work with these few words
while he supposes that he is speaking about the works of
others, almost all of which he describes as falsehoods. Yes,
the author was right in telling us: *the fact of simplifying
breaks communication.* It will be impossible hereafter for
us to accept at face value statements, even Mascolo's, which
do not at the outset admit their partisan unintelligibility.
No longer can we permit ourselves to accord him the confidence which we placed in him spontaneously, just as in

all those, even our adversaries, whom we expect to enlighten us (about ourselves as much as about themselves, on our problems as well as on theirs), a trust that is the first reaction of every sane intellectual. It is by a trick, to boot, and the better to deceive us, that he pretends to consider us as friends and accomplices, us his anonymous readers. In sentences of this kind we are at first aware of a tone of *connivance:* "[Communism is true or nothing is true and] there is nothing left for me or you to do but to suppress ourselves, to commit suicide or at least to keep quiet." Or else this (a vulgarity appears here that we shall come across several times in this author's work): "Life perhaps is not worth living. This question is of no interest. Asked by you and me, intellectual fakers, it is of no interest."

Our author is not astute enough not to appear unintelligent at times. He exposes himself clumsily, suddenly revealing that if he is trying to discredit and discourage us, who are on the opposite side, it is simply because we are not so harmless as he wants to make us believe. He is afraid of us and feels that he, too, is vulnerable, and, no doubt, more so than we are. He admits that he prefers to those who dare to speak about man in general in a non-Communist spirit, those who "withdraw into positions which, in short, are more courageous and can in no way be false, positions of the purely aesthetic elucidation of things." A Communist could not admit more ingenuously that his party has less to fear from a Cocteau than from a Thierry-Maulnier.

But suddenly there are other admissions, deliberate this time, which restore our confidence in Mascolo to the extent that they show that he is aware of his own subterfuges. An uneasiness at first: "The most serious reproach that one could incur would be of having simplified things." Then:

"Most often, to reach the point where one considers something as a definite acquisition is the sign of failure. . . . Speaking here of Marxism, and in support of it, I am surprised. I should never have believed that I would get to the point of speaking in the name of anything at all in the world as if it were something certain. Could it be that my suspicious side has allowed itself to become tired? And would those people be right who said that one's mind cannot remain forever unsubmissive to authority and one must end up either a Communist or a Christian?" He extricates himself nimbly: "It is because Marxism has never tried to impose truth on me. *There is no truth,* those are the first words of Marxism. The Communist movement in its entirety is the exemplification of this phrase."

To make someone doubt, to weaken him, is less to weaken an enemy than to screen him from the real enemy nature, giving him the opportunity to perceive that he is not an enemy. A charity well prescribed: I who am in the very act of saying this am trying thereby to weaken myself first of all. I do it to spoil some part of the assurance, of the health, that enables me to resist much too well, of the resistance that allows me to abide in the midst of falsehood and shame, to tolerate them, to live with them. I don't desire to strengthen myself in some faith or other, only to weaken myself, and to weaken others with me if possible. When our strength is all gone, we shall be happy to put up with the drivel, the pretensions, the all too sad comedy, because we shall be well acquainted with them. One must struggle against all security, all existing moral health.

Mascolo is one of those "who have chosen the search for the Communist truth in its broad lines and who want that choice not to signify the choice of a new way of lying, a falsehood of a new type." I have not yet finished presenting the proofs that he has failed in this laudable objective. The fact remains, nevertheless, that by such a declaration our Communist places himself outside the Communist collectivity and its army, which the Party alone is qualified to represent. "The Communist truth in its broad lines!" What does that mean? To choose not the Communist truth but the search for it? There is a disturbing subtlety here. As for falsehood of a new type, what impudence! And what imprudence! All this smells of the stake and of still further insinuations and assertions—but of the stake voluntarily chosen, which is not without nobility and may some day in retrospect be accepted as a model by the Party itself.

We read elsewhere in the same work: "It is of little importance that at the moment Communism and the aesthetic enterprises that are analogous to it have not historically thrown in their lot with each other, or have done so only for a short time. It is of little importance that Communism even serves as an obstacle to them. Communism has its own contradictions. . . ." On the contrary, it is very important, at least for the writers whose role in and outside of Communism it is Mascolo's purpose to study. Mascolo makes an explicit admission when he says (in passing) that "it is with reason that it seems to modern thought that Communism is the probable destination of the path that everything impels it to follow. It follows it, but does not want Communism; not without reason either." Or else when he notes that there is a new kind of laziness, that of not having the strength to survive as an individual the discovery of the *question of the entirety,* or that "this new type of laziness is destined to flourish in a privileged way in the Communist world." He adds, as though he felt a kind of pleasure in giving ammunition to his adversaries, explaining that Communist society, so long as it continues to be submissive to the economy and to seek theoretical justification, *cannot escape irrationality,* an irrationality in which it tries to justify the Communist practice of *staging extraordinary ruses,* no matter how *comic, unworthy or silly they may be in a certain sense.* Then comes this important passage:

Communism lies, there is no doubt about it. But everything that is not Communist lies even more. Communism is pitiless, there is no doubt about it. But everything that is not Communist is much farther from pity. Communism relies on anything effectual rather than on generosity. But everything that is not Communist is unpardonably lacking in generosity. Finally, sincerity, generosity, pity, which have not assumed the materialist form are only ostentatious and wretched ways for the soul to exercise its faculty for deluding itself.

By the path of heresy, we stumble again upon a pure act of faith. "To be born a bourgeois is to be born in conditions most conducive to contracting a severe case of irrationality. To be a bourgeois means sinking in it to the point of losing one's intelligence." But what about being a Communist? With faith there is fanaticism, born perhaps of a disappointed love. Mascolo does not have sarcasm enough for Christianity. His insults are so bitter that they betray his fright. Whether in the last analysis one can only be either Communist or Christian is a question our author poses, only to evade it immediately. But he is unable to keep from referring to it. Having resolved it as far as he is concerned, he knows that the problem still remains. His vehemence informs us Christianity and Christianity alone is the truly dangerous adversary of Communism. He takes fright at the sight of a cassock. He screams when he comes close to the *consecrated* Christian. Churches, chapels, calvaries, crosses, crucifixes, medals, are for him "signs of the saddest and most basely discouraging obsession that anyone has ever attempted to foist upon man." According to him there exists *a truly sacred duty of irreligion:*

I am not lacking in humility to the point of disdaining the opportunities for profanation that are offered (or rather that provoke) me, since I am in a position every time either to insult or to appear to acquiesce in the wretched holiness the calm performance of which is ostensibly being carried out before my eyes. . . . To the religious man more than to any other, religion must be apparent today in all its aspects and in all its repulsive manifestations of lukewarmness, laziness, and baseness of point of view. Even more, since authentic holiness can find religion to be only the successful result of what makes it a subject of derision, it must consider religion as par excellence that which deserves detestation. It is a grotesque replica of what allows me to go on living and what disfigures holiness. It is scorn of the sacred at its peak.

The insult here is primitive in the sociological sense of the word. No form of holiness can recognize a rival without renouncing itself. We know that Communism is a religion in more than one sense, a religion so young and powerful that it will have to wait a long time before discovering that tolerance for other kinds of faith is possible. Mascolo has just spoken as a religious man about religious men. He has just appealed to the holy. He has shown himself to be a fanatic, not avoiding the most obvious untruths since he is struck with blindness by whatever does not conform to his particular form of irrationality. Listen to him announce the death of Catholicism at a time when the Church has had its greatest revival in a long time:

Of the old religious structure (as in 1789 of the edifice of feudal monarchy) all that remains are empty churches, still standing like large dead trees, obstructing our view, casting shadows, but no longer gripping the earth except with inert roots. Such as they are, we know that they still absorb a great amount of live energy; but it is all for nothing, only to feed oblivion.

But here is a cry—a sign of nostalgia: "It is tiring always to forbid oneself recourse to religious simplification. It is painful not to be able to pray, for example." Described at length is *an annoyance* which has all the characteristics of what others call *the metaphysical disease*. Here at last is something that admits the religious origin of Dionys Mascolo's present faith. Having set out in search of the absolute (which makes him sympathetic to us) he believes that he has found it (for which we envy him):

As a young man, I had been convinced for a long time that men of faith, Christians, were people who had seen God. Not seen him, no doubt, as I saw them. But, in short, they communicated with Him, He manifested Himself to them. . . . I say "young," but I had reached twenty, I think, and I still believed. I was not precocious. It would be curious just the same to see how many men of faith speak plainly enough to allow no doubt to remain on this score. . . . But it left me with a disgust with religious vestments, in particular, which I can best express by saying that they are for me, even today, a sign of the most enormous, most impudent falsehood, most deserving of hate even from a great distance. And this is perhaps a simplification of feeling, but I still have trouble finding myself altogether similar to anyone who does not have this disgust in common with me. But, in brief, I thought that this comedy was true.

Was I wrong in speaking of disappointed love, of restored faith? Denying and again denying all that is not his passion, Dionys Mascolo is not, however, unaware of the weak spot in his book. He happens to let it slip at the turn of a page:

A threat of subtle subversion torments an author without respite, for weighing heavily on his work is the possibility of seeing itself finally marked with a *minus* sign, a possibility he is always aware of, even if only vaguely. . . . From this there is no refuge for anyone. No work, no literary work at any rate, escapes the risk of being influenced by the negative sign which can throw it as far into the minus column as it thought it had risen in the plus. . . . And this concerns all of us, "we" who are looking for something.

By pinning it down to "no literary work, at any rate" is Mascolo trying to exclude himself from the threat of this curse? I don't think so. In spite of its subject, *Le Communisme* is a literary work. This is its charm and its weakness at the same time. Literature is the only area where he feels at ease. He lets this secret out in his preface: "It is because the author, who is neither an economist, sociologist, historian, nor philosopher, but is, nevertheless, anxious to speak about Communism, must start with something . . ." That is, with the position of the writer, or, more generally, the intellectual. His book reveals in Mascolo a constant obsession with what, in his eyes, has even more prestige than Communism: literature. He is obviously from the parish (that of Saint-Germain-des-Prés), knows the passwords, plays the game as naturally as he can, doesn't lack talent, although he writes too quickly (his piece seems dictated), repeats himself, and doesn't know how to cut things short. He writes: "In his room, at his table, one has the feeling of working on the preparations for some terrorist action, manipulating explosives, at the risk, moreover, of being blown up without having had the time to leave the room, as often happens. Of course, this terrorism is theoretical, even literary, if you wish. . . ." It is not that I wish. I simply make the observation that Mascolo is running no risk of being blown up. Much more than that: his book is much too literary to run the risk of blowing up anything at all, not that I deny it a very definite value as apologia. I even believe that he will make some conversions, but to a heterodox Communism, which will seem devoid of any real danger in the eyes of official Communism, inasmuch as it knows that the Party alone is effective. The following passage is not dictated, this time, but written with love. The quotation marks in which Mascolo encloses it are a dodge by which we are not fooled; the author simply wants to win praise for his literary talent without sharing in the discredit of every literary work:

Equivalent propositions when repeated end by causing the most painful confusion: "You know nothing. You understand nothing. You live in darkness as if buried alive. You have seen nothing. Recognized nothing. Learned nothing. You are sixty years old, you have sired six children, you have a life full of works behind you and the first breath of a new spring makes you tremble like a young girl who still expects all from the unknown. You dream. At each awakening you find yourself tossed back on the same desert, run aground in life, a formless wreck, eaten away by boredom, ignorance, absence. There is nothing. You are nothing. And to top it off, if you open your mouth, it is always in order to begin to speak verbatim the sayings of the Word. . . ."

I am not quoting this passage as a joke. We have all been through this kind of thing. But the Communists do not have a very high opinion of men of letters, still less for those of aliterature. They only like their writers submissive. Mascolo himself, who swings back and forth between literature and aliterature like every free writer, does not, it seems, have much respect for Communist men of letters. "To speak without provocation," to borrow one of his sayings (which smacks of fear), Mascolo speaks of the *definite lack of brilliance in Marxist thought.* I still don't know if, in the rest of his essay, he goes as far as Roland Barthes, another "progressive" who hasn't irony enough to judge the petit-bourgeois writing of Communist novelists like Garaudy or André Stil: "A language saturated with convention, which offers the real only in quotation marks." The true "progressive" writers for the author of *Dégré Zéro de l'écriture* (and I understand by that those who make language advance into unknown paths) were, with a few exceptions, the same.

Mascolo does not pick Sartre, of whom Barthes said, in congratulating him: "It is indisputably a victory for Sartre that it has never been said that he wrote well." (There it is, the zero degree of writing!) Dionys Mascolo, on the contrary, finds that "Sartre writes well, even too well not to arouse distrust." Barthes chooses Sartre, Camus, Blanchot, Cayrol, Queneau, while Mascolo cites Bataille, Queneau, Leiris, Blanchot. And I: Bataille, Beckett, Leiris, Michaux. . . . All of us keep lighting on these all but interchangeable names. Now, according to Dionys Mascolo, it is these non-Communist authors who to date have come closest to the ideal of true Communist thought in that they do not lose sight in their writing of what *is missing*, what *is not said*, what *is not known*. One can imagine the reaction of the (true) Communist (false) writers!

Just about all other men of letters are damned by Mascolo: "The uninteresting works of our great writers are non-communications which borrow their style from communication." And that is all very well, from his point of view. Each individual finds what interests him where he wants and where he can. We draw the line when, after being forced to fix his gaze in a precise direction, the observer is required to wear blinkers, so that he is prevented from seeing anything else and is made content not to take it into account at all. "Who ever thought to look in Claudel to find out how to change one's life?" asks Mascolo—putting the names of Verlaine, d'Annunzio and Barrès beside Claudel's in order to steer the reply better. But, beginning with young Jacques Rivière, many individuals who are Mascolo's equals in science and conscience certainly have done so. According to him, in Claudel's work *the faculty of proving anything was amputated*. And he adds: "One wonders how it is possible to admire *Partage de midi*." I wonder how it is possible for anyone who is somewhat intelligent to think and speak so foolishly. Here again is the unintelligence that we have already seen. This is not a peculiarity of M. Mascolo's: it is true of all intellectuals who remain partisan even in the act of understanding. It is true that the author of the work studied here devotes a chapter to his own stupidity. These are admissions about which one has no desire to laugh: "It is impossible to talk of stupidity without talking about oneself." And: "Everyone knows from experience what an ocean of stupidity keeps pounding at the temples of a normal man." Unfortunately, the lucidity of Dionys Mascolo is confined to his past. He was stupid (oh! how stupid he was!) when he was not a Communist. The danger remains today, but it is enough to be on guard against it. Some Communists do not avoid it, that is only too certain: "A trifle would still be enough for the whole building to tumble. . . . Nothing in this domain is acquired once and for all. On the contrary, most often when one reaches the point of considering something as a definite acquisition that is the sign of failure." It happens to many writers, even Communists. One gets the impression that Dionys Mascolo is thinking about Aragon. As for himself, he does not press his usual masochism nor his occasional sense of perfection to the point of considering that the "stupidity of intelligence" with which he has been entertaining us may apply to him right now.

E. M. CIORAN

ONE OF THE BEST FRENCH WRITERS TODAY IS A RUMANIAN in exile. So far, he is known only to a few admirers, who will be followed by many others. This is E. M. Cioran, author of three essays, *Précis de décomposition* (Summary of Decay; 1949), *Syllogismes de l'amertume* (Syllogisms of Bitterness; 1952), and *La Tentation d'exister* (The Temptation to Exist; 1956).

There are few French authors who know how to use our language with such mastery. Cioran, who believes in nothing, can't resist having faith in beautiful language. Attaching importance to words is one of the weaknesses he admits, one of the few breaks in the continuity of his skepticism. For him, the emptiness of the word corresponds to the emptiness of the world. The emptiness hidden by things is found also behind the names designating them: "When, alone in the midst of words, we are incapable of communicating the slightest vibration, and they seem to us as dry, as degraded, as ourselves, when the mind's silence weighs more heavily than that of objects, we descend to the point of being frightened by our own inhumanity. Anchorless, far from our conspicuous truths, we suddenly are filled with a horror for language which throws us into speechlessness—a moment of vertigo when poetry alone can console us for our convictions and our doubts." True. But how well said. . . . Cioran doesn't forgive himself for continuing to write. He belongs to those who, aware that only silence has power, none the less cannot give up the word, especially writing. Cioran, the hopeless, is a man of letters, a contradiction that he feels keenly. It is another opportunity to ridicule himself. While proceeding farther and farther into negation, time after time, within himself, Cioran comes across a bit of attachment to life which he cannot overcome.

No other language than French could have been so effective in his constantly renewed effort toward elucidation. Cioran has *espoused the genius of a language that specializes in sighs of the intellect, in which whatever is not cerebral is suspect or nil.* The very perfection of French indicates its limitations. The author of *La Tentation d'exister* recalls the incapacity of our language to translate the *Iliad* and the Bible, Shakespeare and Cervantes. "The sublime, the horrible, blasphemy or cry, are approached by French only to be denatured in rhetoric." This is good medicine for a foreigner accustomed to idioms whose plasticity gives an impression of unfailing power over a world which, in their attempts at explanation, they make even more obscure. The decadence of the West is particularly perceptible to Cioran. He associates himself with what is destroying little by little the civilization which supports him. France itself does not always escape his blasphemies. This wicked lucidity, this refusal to have hope in the future, this lack of indulgence, E. M. Cioran turns first of all against himself. It is a new opportunity to sink a little deeper into negation. By indicting what he loves, he hurts himself a little more. We might say he gives himself a little more pleasure; he is masochistic. No one can attain total indifference toward the world and himself. By reopening his wounds Cioran maintains a feeling of sensuality that makes peace of mind impossible for him as well as for others. In the preface to a selection of his writings, he admires Joseph de Maistre for heaping scorn "on the method of attacking God by revolt, jeering or despair." His power of execration fascinates him: "It was an imperative, a condition indispensable to the fecundity of his imbalance; without it, he might have fallen into sterility, the curse of thinkers who will not condescend to cultivate their disagreements with others or with themselves." Cioran knows what and whom he is talking about.

The author of *Le Tentation d'exister* thinks constantly about how to humiliate and trample on himself, and not without a secret pride: "Anxious to be covered with ignominy, I envied all who exposed themselves to the sarcasm and venom of others, and who, piling shame on shame, missed no opportunity for solitude. I thus reached the point of idealizing Judas. . . ." He often associates the word "voluptousness" with defeat, weakness, bitterness, and decay. It pleases him to destroy himself. He wishes us rare joys, queer delights:

One day, who knows, perhaps you will experience the pleasure of aiming at an idea, shooting it, seeing it lie there, and then begin the exercise over again on another; on all of them; the desire to bend over an individual, to make him deviate from his old appetites, from his old vices, in order to impose new and more harmful ones on him so that he will perish from them; to become furious at a period or against a civilization, to rush at time and make martyrs of its moments; then, to turn against yourself, to torture your memories and ambitions, and, fouling your breath, infect the air the better to suffocate.

These dream illnesses are born of real anxieties, which in all probability are not all moral ones. He who evokes the lack of air so effectively and so many times must have suffocated already. As for the masochism, we find it tinged as usual with sadism. Cioran considers "our blood too tepid, our appetites too well mastered." He likes the fact that Christianity "at its good moments" was sanguinary, that it *excelled in massacre.* Vandalism charms him. The hysteria of the Middle Ages (or what he so labels) appears admirable to him. As for the anchorites, he envies them for having known so well how *to remedy the insufficiency of their troubles:* "Left to itself, the flesh encloses us in a contracted horizon. As we submit it to torture, it sharpens our perceptions and enlarges our perspectives: the mind is the result of the tortures it undergoes or inflicts." Torture! There is the great anticipated word. We find it in many of our authors. Cioran explains:

We, simple mortals, who cannot permit ourselves the luxury of being cruel to others, should exercise and assuage our terrors upon ourselves, on our own flesh and spirit. The tyrant in us trembles: he must act, get rid of his rage, avenge himself; and he avenges himself on us. So wills the modestness of our condition. In the midst of our terrors, more than one of us evokes a Nero, who, lacking an empire, has only his own conscience to bully and torture.

A vicious circle: masochism again. Cioran dreams then "of an acid thought which would insinuate itself into things to disorganize them, perforate, traverse them; of a book whose syllables, infecting the paper, would eliminate literature and readers; of a book which would be the carnival and apocalypse of Letters, an ultimatum to the pestilence of the Word." A new theoretician of aliterature, he none the less continues his painstaking work.

With France exhausting itself more and more in the midst of a civilization itself in decay (as Cioran claims and we accept his postulate), its language cannot escape degeneration. The author of *La Tentation d'exister* quotes these words of Joseph de Maistre: "All individual or national deterioration is immediately anticipated by a directly proportionate deterioration in language." About this deterioration E. M. Cioran writes some beautiful passages. Assuring us that French is declining, he proves the contrary by the beauty, precision, and cadence of a language which, even in classical times, was scarcely more perfect or efficient. We can say about him what he assures us about La Bruyère: that the semicolon was his obsession. If he uses it with artistry, he employs the exclamation point as rarely as possible, a recourse abused by the romantics.

That it is a Rumanian who handles the French language with such perfection may reassure the French, who might be disturbed or even hurt by the severity of Cioran's views about their country, a severity from which not only is no nation exempt (with the exception of the Jewish people) but nothing else in the world either, not even the world itself or his own country. This is said for the sake of those who might be disagreeably surprised by lines like these: "A nation's bad habits are as apparent as an individual's." Or again: "A nation of the gesture, a theatrical nation, France loved its acting as well as its audience. She has had her fill, she wants to leave the stage, and no longer aspires to anything but the *stage setting of oblivion.*" This is open to argument, but because of his love for the theater Cioran is almost a naturalized citizen, he is one of us. He, too, has a tendency to pose. He has no objection to forcing his ideas a little if the cadences of a fine phrase demand it.

Only the Jews escape, then, from the declaration of failure which our author draws up with a pleasure too grating not to be desperate. The chapter that he devotes to them, *Un peuple de solitaires* (A Nation of Solitaries), is one of the most beautiful in *La Tentation d'exister.* Nothing so intelligent or thorough has ever been written about this unfortunate and admirable race. It pained Cioran to belong to a nation without history. "How can one be a Rumanian?" was a question, he assures us, that he could only answer with perpetual mortification. "Hating my people, my country, its eternal peasants delighted with their torpor and almost bursting with stupidity, I blushed that I was descended from them, disclaimed them, refused to allow myself to accept their sub-eternity, their petrified larval convictions, their geological dreaming." His country, *whose existence obviously made no sense, seemed to him an epitome of non-being and a materialization of the inconceivable:* "To be part of it, what humiliation and irony! What a calamity! What leprosy!" Subsequently, Cioran became reconciled to Rumania, a connivance and complicity which, instead of raising them both, lowered them even more in his estimation. To his country, Cioran owes not only his *peasant neurasthenia,* not only "his finest, surest defeats, but even his gift for covering his cowardice with make-up, for hoarding his remorse," a gift which we know (and he knows) he has all too great a tendency towards: "I realized the advantage of belonging to a small country, of living with no background, carefree as a buffoon, an idiot or a saint. . . ." Elsewhere, pretending to evoke Joseph de Maistre, he tells us a very personal secret: "A thinker enriches himself by everything that escapes him, everything that is hidden from him: if he happens to lose his country, what a piece of luck!"

But Cioran found someone more unfortunate (and more *exiled*) than he: "To be a man is one tragedy; to be a Jew is another. So, the Jew has the privilege of living through our situation *twice*." It pleases him that Jews are unbeatable at jokes. He likes the idea that decadence doesn't bother them, since their history unfolds outside of History. A dead town is a town without Jews. Man is a Jew *who has not made the grade*. The Germans detested in the Jew the realization of their own dreams, the universality which they were unable to attain. Whatever they do and wherever they go, the mission of the Jews is to be on the lookout. In short, although they are in the world, they are really not of it. . . . At last they are trying to take their place in History and to escape "their immemorial status of stranger." E. M. Cioran, who never speaks other than of himself even when he comments on, sings about, and glorifies the great Jewish sorrow, Cioran, for whom there is no other secret or fate but his own, for he is one of those who are fascinated by their own death and can never think about anything else, Cioran confesses that he is grateful to "these vanquishers of the abyss" for having made him glimpse the advantage of not losing his grip, not giving way *to the voluptuousness of being a dere-*

lict: "Meditating on their refusal to be shipwrecked, one vows to imitate them, knowing that it is a vain aspiration, that our lot is to sink to the bottom, to answer the call of the abyss."

When one is ready to capitulate, what a lesson, what a reprimand, their endurance is! How many times, as I stewed over my ruin, have I not thought of their obstinacy, their headstrongness, their appetite for being, as comforting as it is unexplainable! I am indebted to them for many tacks, for many compromises with the disproofs of living.

His appetite for being persisted, no matter how hard he tried to destroy everything solid that he had, while facing the certainty of non-being. Hence the final effort which gave the book its title, the acceptance of the inextinguishable, unsmotherable, unkillable *temptation to exist.* Utterly tired of "polemics with non-being," Cioran aspires *to regain the privileges of irrationality,* privileges, in fact, whose secrets he had never lost completely. "Existing is a habit which he does not despair of acquiring." Consolidating his position with his reverses, he makes believe that he is choosing what is forced upon him: an unuprootable hope. This is the struggle of a moribund man against death. We are all dying. We never stop. Cioran's struggle is the more ours according as we are of his lucid breed.

For it is a breed, and one that has many representatives. There are many of us who have renounced what Cioran calls the superstition of the Ego. Although we don't stop "leaning on ourselves for support," we no longer rehash "our differences." We know that nothing essential distinguishes us, that we are interchangeable, scarcely more or less intelligent than one another. As a result we all write the same books. To quote Cioran is to offer the best possible commentary on the modern novel or essay, Beckett's as well as Camus's. We find again the very words which we all use and which will carry our dearest, cruelest convictions. First and foremost, it should be understood that *we are nothing:*

In revenge for our shortcomings in naïveté, freshness, hope, and simplicity, the "psychological sense," our greatest acquisition, has transformed us into spectators of ourselves. Our greatest acquisition? No doubt it is, taking into account our metaphysical incapacity, just as it is no doubt the only kind of depth of which we are capable. But if one goes beyond psychology, our whole "inner life" assumes the aspect of an emotional meteorology whose variations have no significance. Why be interested in the maneuvers of ghosts, in stages of semblance? . . . The "ego" is essentially the privilege only of those who do not make the most of their capabilities. . . . Suddenly, beyond everything, I glide toward the point of non-existence of each object. The ego: a label.

This results in a new conception of literature, or rather aliterature, which, from Beckett to Robbe-Grillet, through many more obscure researchers, and through Cioran, is in the process of renovating the act of writing. The time of futility is past, and also that of a certain professorial seriousness. In a period often devoid of religious faith, there are no longer any interesting writers except for philosophers. The novelist devotes himself exclusively to an essential that he knows to be relative and misleading, but whose appearance, the only reality within reach, fascinates him. "To reflect life in its details, to degrade our amazement into anecdotes, what a torture for the mind!" So, as far as possible, there is a refusal to concede to the picturesque, to poetry, to the sentimental. The very shadow of Valéry's marquise seems a concession to the novelist of today. No doubt he will be unable to avoid similar, or even less pardonable, descriptions. The trap to catch the impalpable must have a framework. One must also be read and understood. Are three readers enough?

Cioran writes: "An artist describes best what he might have accomplished. He becomes his own critic." And further: "Also it is not without significance that the only novels worthy of interest are precisely those in which, once the universe is dismissed, nothing happens." True. But from here on I no longer agree with him as to novels "delightfully unreadable, without head or tail; they could just as well stop at the first sentence as contain tens of thousands of pages":

A narration that eliminates what is narrated, the object, corresponds to a paroxysm of the intellect, a meditation *without content*. The mind sees itself reduced to the act by which it is mind and nothing more. All its activities lead back to itself, to a stationary unfolding that prevents it from clinging to things. No knowledge, no action. . . .

This *adventure in the unintelligible* does not tempt us. We preserve our yearning for understanding, for grasping. Hence our attention to objects that we refuse to excommunicate, following Robbe-Grillet's example. Hence our need to cling to things, at least to their appearances—and (but here Robbe-Grillet is no longer with us) to those other reflections, thoughts, born of sensations, which they command and comment upon. "*Meaning* begins to be dated." It is on this point that we believe it necessary to part with Cioran and from certain writers whom he salutes without naming. "If the artist of today takes refuge in the obscure, it is because he can no longer innovate *with what he knows*." Before Joyce and Proust this was already asserted. Well, Proust and

Joyce came. Others will come. I shall not give up the idea of seeing and knowing more in what we already see and know.

Therefore, we reaffirm that even for the *alittérateurs* everything ends in literature. . . . Cioran denies the outer world, denouncing its unreality, scrutinizing his obsession with death, then, in the end, offers his despair a hope, even if it is false. But he never stops coming back to language problems. And I myself, reviewing his work, stress its literary character still more by dwelling on what refers only to the question of style. It is because in a universe where truth is dead, nothing consoles us, nothing amuses us, except the lullaby which we sing to ourselves and which can only be made of words. They are what Cioran, the metaphysician of non-being, calls *the axioms of twilight*.

A.
ROBBE-GRILLET

ALAIN ROBBE-GRILLET IS THE FORERUNNER OF A REVOLUTION in the novel more radical than Romanticism and Naturalism were in their time. This almost unknown form, he tells us, is already trying to establish itself in spite of resistance all the way from publishers to the most modest readers "via the bookseller and the critic." Renouncing "sacrosanct psychological analysis," and, as far as possible, the subjective point of view, it tries to reflect the world as it is: neither significant nor absurd, just present. "Around us, defying the pack of our life-giving or frugal adjectives, things are *there*. Their surface is clean and smooth, *intact,* but without false brilliance or transparency. All of our literature has not yet even cut the smallest corner or made a dent in it." The result is that in the future world of the novel, *actions and objects will be "there" before being "something."* This bewildering appearance of a world impervious to any frame of reference whatsoever ("sentimental, sociological, Freudian, metaphysical or other") is found by Alain Robbe-Grillet to be much more plainly revealed in the cinema than in the present-day novel. It is found not only in the avant-garde cinema but in the filmed equivalents of mediocre novels, where the most conventional scenario does not interfere with the well-named objective of disclosing common objects in all their bareness. On the screen, any chair photographed by any cameraman easily becomes Van Gogh's chair:

It may seem bizarre that these fragments of raw reality, which the cinematographic story can't help presenting without realizing it, impress us to such a degree, while identical scenes in daily life are not enough to cure us of our blindness. Everything happens, in fact, as if the conventions of photography (the two dimensions, black and white, the frame, the difference in scale between foreground and background) contribute to freeing us from our own conventions. The somewhat unusual appearance of this "reproduced" world reveals to us, at the same time, the *unusual* character of the world around us: unusual, to the extent that it refuses to yield to our habits of perception and order.

With a few exceptions, of which we shall speak, one can only agree with such observations. Alain Robbe-Grillet seems somewhat unjust to the publishers (he was understood and defended by M. Jérôme Lindon, head of Éditions de Minuit, who publish him as well as Beckett and a few other authors who are expected to find their public in the future). He is unjust to the critics, too, not only because they awarded their prize to his second novel after having favorably mentioned the first, but because in the books they receive they are looking precisely for *the features of that new novel* of which I myself spoke some time ago in an article, in connection with two young authors, Claude Simon and Charles Duits. It seemed to me that what characterized the views of the best novelists with this tendency was a certain way of describing the so-called objective world in the changing relief and the shifting density of its appearances. I added that it would not surprise me if this manner of seeing and describing things did not have the cinema, not, to be sure, as its source, but as its stimulus.

Novelists and critics of a certain school have all been working in the same direction for several years. Alain Robbe-Grillet has not only formulated his objectives in a fortunate way, he has applied his theories and proved that the novel of the future is possible by writing novels today which are already more than forerunners of what is to come.

Alain Robbe-Grillet disregards the feelings and complicated thoughts of his heroes. All that counts is the immediate sensation. Man is reduced to a robot, the mind to a recording machine, so no incident is of more importance than another. The mission of the detective in *Gommes* disappears in the accumulation of actions (and steps) necessary to accomplish it. The author does not spare any details, and all details are on the same plane for his hero. To quote him is difficult. Here is how a closing drawbridge comes to rest before the fascinated gaze of the detective:

But on the other side of the barrier it was clear that all was not over: because of a certain elasticity of the mass, the descent of the flooring had not come to an end when the mechanism stopped; it continued for a few seconds, for a centimeter, perhaps, creating a slight break in the continuity of the roadway; a tiny rising took place, which in its turn brought the metallic edge a few millimeters above its position of equilibrium; and the oscillations, dying down more and more, becoming less and less discernible— it was difficult to find the exact term—shook, thus, like a fringe in a series of successive extensions and regressions on either side of an entirely illusory stability; for a noticeable time, however, a phenomenon had been consummated.

I have given the reader only the end of the description, having dispensed with a great number of pages devoted to the same bridge which the hero often crosses in the course of his police peregrinations, and which we have to see every time he does. Never is anything hidden. No distraction. Thought and its images have their reality, nevertheless. We are already exposing the weak spot in Robbe-Grillet's too-exclusive theory. The process of reasoning is as real as a reaction. A thought is just as indicative as nausea. I can suffer through the mind as well as through the senses. Fear of the abuses of sacrosanct psychological analysis leads this author to the opposite extreme. Thoughts, subtle or not, are no more or less veracious than objects, useful or not. The existence of a psychological change is just as indisputable as a physical displacement. It cannot be claimed that the reactions of the body are less misleading than those of the mind. Here is another example taken from *Gommes:*

Eight short and fat fingers pass and repass over each other delicately, the backs of four fingers against the inside of the four left ones. The left thumb caresses the nail of the right, at first gently, then rubbing more and more. The other fingers change their positions . . .

That's enough. These few lines allow one to imagine those that follow. For the same reason, I shall give up the idea of reproducing the description of a post office, which is reduced to the reading of *all* the signs over the windows. It begins with "PAYMENTS. STAMPS WHOLESALE" and ends with "GENERAL DELIVERY. STAMPS RETAIL," with about fifteen interven-

ing lines (PARCEL POST, POSTAL SAVINGS, TELEGRAMS, etc.).
The same method is similarly applied in *Le Voyeur:*

> There was then, starting from the window and turning to the
> left (or counterclockwise) : a chair, a second chair, the dressing
> table (in the corner), a clothespress, a second clothespress (reach-
> ing the second corner), a third chair, the cherry-wood bed placed
> lengthwise against the wall; a very small table in front of a
> fourth chair, a commode (in the third corner), the door to the
> corridor, a kind of secretary with its leaf raised, and finally the
> third clothespress occupying at an angle the fourth corner, in
> front of the fifth and sixth chairs.

The minutiae in the description interfere with the view. One
sees no better for seeing more. Actually, we seem to grasp
more of the over-all than of the details. To decide the contrary is perhaps an assumption as good as any. But by what
right could it be called less conventional? At the start of
every creative work there is a plan. There is no art without
choice. The author of *Gommes* and *Le Voyeur* gives the impression at first of making no choice in what is presented to
him. Then one becomes aware of the plan: to keep what has
no importance to the action of the novel and make it the
fictional material itself. Small facts that novelists ordinarily
neglect but that the novel takes for granted: changes of
place minutely described, with the houses and streets always
the same and practically interchangeable. Machinelike con-
versations of the class: "Winter is coming," the theme of a
frosty morning. Choosing the unessential, the author is still
making a choice. Why should this method give us any better
insight into what is existential in appearances? Toward the
end of *Gommes* we read: "He follows the circular boulevard
which leads him back to the little brick pavilion. . . Wallas is

no farther ahead than he was yesterday when he arrived by the same road." Nor is the reader.

The universe exists only through us. The objects that Robbe-Grillet wishes to describe with the least possible subjectivity keep the names with which we associate them. As for nature's gifts, they, too, remain as man sees them and not as they really are. There is a contradiction between the passivity expected of this recording glance and the activity which the minuteness of view presupposes. Alain Robbe-Grillet reconstructs what he describes:

Between them and the table—taking up the whole length of the latter, but hidden from sight by it—there was the bench. The room as a whole was thus cut up into a network of parallel elements: the back wall, first, against which were found, on the right, the stove, then some boxes, and on the left, in the half light, a larger piece of furniture; in the second place, at an indefinite distance from the wall, the line indicated by the man and his wife; after that came, still going toward the front: the invisible bench, the broad axis of the rectangular table—which passes through the oil lamp and the opaque bottle—finally, the windowframe.

A geometric universe which has reality only through a man's glance. The detective in *Gommes* loses his way one morning when the fog gives distances "a new quality no longer related to geometry." The hero of *Le Voyeur*, too, moves in a world made of angles, lines and parallels. He is busy looking at a milestone of the ordinary type, "a parallelopiped rectangle attached to a semicylinder of the same thickness (and with a horizontal axis)." The description continues, but what's the use: the reader knows what a milestone is. It pleases Robbe-Grillet that the scales of a wall become detached in polygonal fragments. He feels the need to note that a certain little plaza is not strictly rectangular: rather it forms a trapezium. He feels better, now that that is settled. The flame of a lamp appears to him to be in the form of a very jagged triangle with two branches, whose lack of symmetry he regrets, we feel. Finally, here are two eyes, neither ugly nor beautiful, neither large nor small, "two perfect and immobile circles, situated side by side and each one pierced in the center by a black hole." Such objectivity, it seems to me, betrays the person looking much more than a more human observation.

In this way Alain Robbe-Grillet applies himself to the task of changing literary language. Nothing is more contrived than his art. His manifesto ends with this profession of faith:

We ascertain from day to day in those who are most conscious an increasing repugnance for words of a visceral, analogical, or magical character. Meanwhile the optical, descriptive adjective, the one that is content to measure, situate, limit, define, is probably showing the difficult path to a new fictional art.

We have pointed out what, according to us, are the faults of this conception, which, applied even more arbitrarily if possible in *La Jalousie* (Jealousy), finds its justification in its very lack of moderation. Psychology is reborn, new, bare and pure from its destruction. Never, perhaps, has the insane character of jealousy been made perceptible with such acuteness. The heroine, although she is not described with any of the usual words, is surprisingly *seductive*. For the first time, in convincing fashion, Alain Robbe-Grillet gives us a beautiful and genuine novel in *La Jalousie*. No doubt his theories will prove fruitful when they become more flexible through use and are reconciled with what should be kept from the fictional assets of the past. There is no doubt that he has already advanced quite far in the right direction.

With or without him, the same holds true of a few other novelists whose personal research is analogous, and some of whom, having started out without companions, discovered in the middle of their journey that they were not alone.

Alain Robbe-Grillet's universe resembles no other. This "Einsteinian mixture of time and space" (to take Roland Barthes' definition) bewilders the reader less than it brings to him a forgotten, rejected experience—obsessive again: a world where man has no place and where he must adapt himself. Objects here have the disturbing effect of unmanageable things.

Just as in all the great cubists, so also some beautiful still lifes will be found in the writings of the author of *La Voyeur*, a weakness, no doubt, a brief concession to the picturesque. (Robbe-Grillet writes in his manifesto: "In the midst of the sincere praise, most of it will be offered to vestiges of times elapsed, to bonds that my work has not yet broken and which desperately draw it backward.") One will discover fixed plans similar to those introduced purposely by scenarists in their sets. And one will admire in *Gommes* a description of a quarter of a tomato which combines the precision dear to Robbe-Grillet with plastic beauty, indeed with poetry, which he distrusts.

This roughhewn universe is more complex than one thinks. As elementary as it is, the intervention of the *voyeur* transforms the solid world of things into an evanescent world of thought. It is a disproportionate amount of work for a mind faced with imaginary difficulties, or, just the opposite, unable to conceive a reality that is too large for its faculties to absorb. On-the-spot reports of churning thought. Flashes of ideas gone at once and their traces soon after. For Robbe-Grillet's heroes, too, and in a particularly baffling way, the scene is often inside a person who pays no attention to it. Or the author does not warn us that the inconsistent images from the past have taken precedence over the tangible ones of the present. There is less inner dialogue than inner acting-out. But Robbe-Grillet's characters don't act as if they were in the movies: filmed fragments of their past roll by in snatches within them, mixed indistinctly with moving snapshots of the present. It is up to the reader to find them. It will be less difficult because all modern aliterature since Joyce has accustomed him to this type of mental gymnastics.

What is new in Robbe-Grillet (or rather what would be new without the precedent of Francis Ponge), is the concrete character of the images, whether they are caught by a glance or seen again in the darkroom of the mind. He deliberately uses in his novels the revealing difference mentioned by him between reality and its cinematographic representation. It is then not only his heroes but their creator himself who makes movies—avant-garde movies and novels. No doubt Robbe-Grillet is a pioneer. It is possible that he has found a way out of the impasse which the most advanced literature had reached—so that it was no longer advancing. After Kafka, we saw Antonin Artaud, Michel Leiris, Samuel Beckett, Georges Bataille, Albert Camus, Henri Michaux, each footing it along at the pace suitable to him, trying in vain, each in his own way, to embrace an obsessive and imperceptible reality. By grasping objects visually without judging them, being satisfied to take them without wanting to understand, Alain Robbe-Grillet escapes perhaps, and perhaps makes literature escape inanity. This fictional study of phenomena is itself mis-leading, but it is capable of giving an illusion some of the time, thus making possible works that will be something more than proof of impotence or madness. Movement is proved by walking. It is enough that the disabused, suspicious men who are the writers of today admit that there is a motive for moving. Alain Robbe-Grillet offers them the possibility of escaping. Be faithful to your view, be nothing but your view. It is important to add: and to that deeper view which, within you, watches you watching.

NATHALIE SARRAUTE

ACCORDING TO NATHALIE SARRAUTE IN HER *L'Ere du Soupçon* (Era of Suspicion), the word "psychology" is one that no author today can hear mentioned in connection with himself *without lowering his eyes and blushing*. She herself makes the assertion without lowering her eyes or blushing, with the aplomb of one who is expressing a truth that has passed into the public domain. But it is the assurance of a writer loudly dissociating herself from that of which she knows she is an accomplice, if not indeed guilty herself.

"No author"? That is not at all exact, if only by virtue of the attention some of us still pay to psychology, a word we no longer need to put in quotation marks or underline, while at the same time we recoil from it somewhat with a kind of disdain. The orthodoxy that Mme. Sarraute wishes here to represent, however, finds in her a defender who is suspect. There are many among us who want to reintroduce psychology into the modern novel without, on the contrary, having it lose any of its power. After some strange detours, Nathalie Sarraute herself finally concurs with this in *L'Ere du Soupçon,* which does not surprise us when we remember that she is the author of the most psychological stories possible, which are, none the less, new. I am thinking about those amazing books which pile up pages of psychological riches: *Tropismes, Portrait d'un inconnu* (Portrait of Man Unknown), *Martereau, Le Planétarium.* Whoever reads *L'Ere du Soupçon* without keeping the novels of Nathalie Sarraute in mind will not avoid the misconception of seeing an indictment in what is, for anyone who is not duped by appearances, a speech for the defense.

For most of us, the author of *L'Ere du Soupçon* says, expressing herself this time a little more prudently (she no longer claims that it is the case with *all* authors today), "the works of Joyce and Proust already stand in the distance like witnesses to a period that has ended." Joyce? "He drew out of the obscure depths of the human being only an uninterrupted unrolling of words." That is not badly said. And not without courage, for one must be audacious indeed today to dare to have the least reservation about Joyce or Kafka. Proust? Let us be careful here to read attentively judgments that come (one should not forget) from the most Proustian, the only real Proustian, perhaps, of today's novelists, Nathalie Sarraute being, to my mind, the only living author who has created anything new after Proust. We shall discover, then, that the author of *A la recherche du temps perdu* rarely, virtually never, tried to make his characters live again "in the present while they are taking shape and as they are being developed like so many minuscule dramas, each having its vicissitudes, its mystery, and its unforeseeable dénouement." It was not in search of the present that Marcel Proust started out. . . . Mme. Sarraute is not unaware of this, but she remembers still better the theories on the novel of Jean-Paul Sartre (who wrote a preface to her novel: *Portrait d'un inconnu*). What is best in *Martereau* finds its source in Proust, the less good—the combination of images frequently evoked by what others are thinking—having its origin partially in Sartre.

Thus the author of *L'Ere du Soupçon, tacitly* referring to her own efforts in the novel and her personal discoveries, has the right to reproach the creator of *Swann* for having "in the most new parts of his work, incited the reader to make his intellect function, instead of having given him the sensation of reliving an experience, and without knowing too well what he is doing or where he is going, accomplishing actions himself—which has always been and still is the proper function of every work in the novel form." True, Proust's descriptions of his characters are in the highest degree evocative:

But those innumerable and minute movements which prepare the dialogues are, for Proust, in the place from which he observes them, what the waves and whirlpools in the watercourse are for the cartographer who studies a region as he flies over it; he sees and reproduces only the large motionless lines composed by these movements, the points where these lines are joined, crossed, or separated; he recognizes among them those that have already been explored and designates them with their known names: jealousy, snobbery, fear, modesty, etc.; he describes, classifies, and names those which he has discovered; he tries to extract from his observations some general principles.

The result is that the insignificant particles of almost impalpable matter gathered by the author of *A la recherche du temps perdu* "stick to one another, amalgamate into a coherent whole, with very precise contours, in which the trained eye of the reader immediately recognizes a rich man of the world in love with a kept woman, a successful doctor, gullible and thickheaded, a parvenu bourgeois woman or a snobbish woman of the world, who will join in his imaginary museum a whole vast collection of fictional characters." And Nathalie Sarraute concludes with conscious impertinence (one must make one's self understood and she knows that the admirable Proust is beyond attack) : "How much trouble to arrive at results which, without contortions and hair-splitting, are obtained by, let us say, Hemingway." Read *Martereau* before smiling. One of the characters in the *Planétarium* thinks:

The language has not yet been discovered that can explain at a single stroke what one perceives in a blink of the eye: a whole being and his myriads of little movements surging forth in a few words, a gesture, a sneer. . . .

Yes, it has, and Nathalie Sarraute knows it better than anyone else, since this is her great novelistic conquest: the domain of dizzy individual inanity, the domain we all know, our coenesthesic and social existence.

In the modern novel, this means revealing to the reader, as they unfold, subterranean manifestations which are more and more complex or more and more elementary, but always buried more deeply. Nathalie Sarraute draws attention to the fact that the secrets of those obscure recesses of the being are not disclosed by our actions. The most subtle of these appear coarse compared with those delicate and minute inner forces. For a long time their conformations and motivations have been known and classified: "heavy, very visible ropes that make all of this enormous and weighty machinery work":

It is these heavy mobiles, these very apparent vast movements, and only they, that ordinarily are seen by authors and readers, carried away by the movement of the action and spurred on by the plot, in behavioristic novels. They have neither the time nor the means—having at their disposal no instrument of investigation delicate enough—to see in detail the finer and more fugitive movements which these great movements hide. Thus one understands the repugnance which these authors feel for what they call "analysis," which would amount to making these large mobiles visible, doing the work for their readers, and giving themselves the disagreeable impression of breaking down open doors.

But what about locked doors? Those that call for finer and finer and more and more complicated keys? Far from condemning analysis, we should, on the contrary, devote the best of our intelligence and patience to it, so as to make it more and more precise and meticulous. Even after Proust, even after Joyce, it should be repeated, what remains to be discovered is limitless. Possibly, the first stage of the future may be precisely to unite and reconcile in the same novel the discoveries of Proust and those of Joyce, Proust being considered here as the last link in the long chain of the French novel, Joyce as the first link in the chain of modern writers. But this future, Nathalie Sarraute and a few others, but especially Nathalie Sarraute, have already partially made into a present.

Similarly, the author of the *Planétarium*, as I have pointed out, ends by contradicting herself and rehabilitating that psychology for which, no doubt, she had only feigned disdain in order to rescue it. It is indeed true, she says, that Stendhal and Tolstoi are being rewritten indefinitely, while Joyce and Proust cannot be rewritten. This is, first of all, because the moderns have transferred the essential interest in the novel elsewhere: "For them it is no longer found in the enumeration of situations and characters or in the painting of manners, *but in bringing new psychological matter to light. It is the discovery of this matter, even if only a few particles of it, an anonymous matter found in all men and in all society, that constitutes the true revival."*

It is we who have done the underlining, happy to hear Nathalie Sarraute at last speak the language we expected from the author of *Martereau,* where there are offered to us many particles, we may even say golden particles, of this matter. The critic of *L'Ere du Soupçon* adds that to rework the same dough after Joyce and Proust, without modifying anything in their methods, would be as absurd as to begin *Le Rouge et le Noir* or *War and Peace* again with the same characters and the same plots. But it is in the direction indicated by Joyce and Proust that the best novelists of tomorrow (and already, to a considerable extent, Mme. Sarraute today) will advance, going farther than they if possible. Or at the very least, visiting the regions that they neglected to explore, having gone beyond them without stopping. It is the lowly domain of everyday psychology that Proust left to the novelist of *Martereau,* for after Proust we can be no more than gleaners of nothings. But these nothings are none the less rich. The analysis in *L'Ere du Soupçon* of *wounding words* [pp. 102ff.] has its counterpart in *Martereau,* as well as many other dramas of the same kind, small but decisive. It is in these regions of sensitivity known but neglected by all, that Nathalie Sarraute's analysis is practiced. Analysis in the traditional sense, except that it registers all perceptible details and even those very ones that are generally imperceptible. A few examples are necessary here. I have taken them from *Martereau,* but I could just as well have chosen them from any other book of our author:

She felt something, that is certain . . . she suspected something
. . . she is watching me . . . underneath she did not stop spying
upon me while she had the air of chattering away innocently, of
wallowing about without a care, when I believed myself to be in
such security, behind closed doors, guarded on every side—but in
spite of all precautions, efforts, one can never succeed in fooling
them—she suddenly became aware, she noticed something, a vibration, less than a breath, a motion at the corner of my lips,
in my glance a wavering, she understood. . . . [p. 15]

. . . And all of a sudden, in the heart of the exquisite feeling of
intimacy, of nascent friendship, of unhoped-for rapprochement,
something arises in him, a little icy breath, a doubt which he
hardly dares formulate—how can one believe that there is so
much cynicism in them, so much hypocritical coldness, so extreme
a feeling of hierarchy—something arises to which he will never
give full citizenship, or only much later, one of those half-hatreds
of the most dangerous kind, one of those shameful rancors, hectic,
almost impossible to satiate.

But, between her and me, it was not that, surely, not that at all.
It had slipped into me, an echo, a reflection, less than a remi-
niscence, a vague recollection of something that I had perhaps not
experienced myself but seen, read about somewhere, caught a
glimpse of, brushed against, sniffed, I don't know too well where
or when. It was rather, during the time she spoke, something like
the advance point of a far-off land, a promontory which had suddenly appeared to me favored by a brief break in the clouds, for
just an instant I perceived it and it disappeared, was effaced.
[p. 20]

In *Martereau,* many acute and fugitive passages correspond
to feelings or even sensations that have not yet been named.
I have christened them *sarrauteries,* for my personal use.
This nonexistence, or this incapacity for words, is one of
the *leitmotivs* of *Martereau,* and shows their power of camou-
flage or, on the contrary, of explosion.

They are sure of impunity, well protected, entrenched behind
their words. Nobody could succeed in attaching himself to the

smooth rampart of their speech and reach them up there where they are, lurking like cowards and spying on us, protected behind their rampart, from whence they shower us with pitch and boiling oil. [p. 120]

Words are not for him what they are for me—thin protecting capsules which cover noxious germs, but hard and full objects, of a single mold; in vain would one open them up, dissect them, examine them, one would discover nothing there. [p. 133]

"And then . . . you say nothing . . . what's new? . . . what are you making that's beautiful? . . ." almost nothing, banal formulas, meaningless words, but there are no meaningless words between us, there are no more meaningless words, words that are tiny safety valves through which heavy gases, unhealthy emanations, escape, surround me. . . . [p. 283]

Thus does Nathalie Sarraute analyze in *Martereau* "all those would-be bites, those attacks, those low blows, that no one else receives, notices, about which no one ever speaks, bothers, from which no one ever thought to teach anybody to defend himself." The author, like her hero, "likes those lowly nuances where now and then lies the truth." True, we are often disappointed by what is brought up from the depths: "Tempests in teapots are my great speciality," confesses the narrator. But for our glance at her work today, for Nathalie Sarraute, at this moment in her research, these lowly details are all that Proust left for her to gather. Such is the Proustian impregnation that the hero of *Martereau* resembles the narrator of the *Recherche* even in his real and imaginary ills: "It is for the sake of my health that I am here, for obvious reasons of health, on the advice of doctors, that I lead this somewhat padded life, in slow motion. . . ."

Nathalie Sarraute, then, disdains psychology all the less in that she, more than any other novelist today, excels in this field. Someone in *Martereau* sneers about psychology, but it is certainly not the narrator. Mme. Sarraute herself ends by admitting this in *L'Ere du Soupçon:*

However, despite these rather serious reproaches that can be made about analysis, it is difficult to ignore it without turning one's back on progress. Would it not be better to try, notwithstanding all possible obstacles and disappointments, to perfect an instrument to be used for new research, which, perfected in its turn by new men, will permit them to describe new situations and feelings in a more convincing way, with more truth and life, rather than to adjust oneself to methods that seize what is only the appearance, and that tend to fortify still more the natural penchant of everyone for the *trompe-l'œil?*

Mme. Sarraute dreams, then, of a technique that would succeed in plunging the reader into the stream of those subterranean dramas which Proust *only had time to skim over,* and of which he was able *to observe and reproduce only the broad motionless lines.* Observations and skimmings with which we would be satisfied! What genius it would take to give the reader (as Mme. Sarraute wishes, without too many illusions) the impression of reaccomplishing those actions himself, with more consciousness, lucidity, order, precision, clarity than is possible in life, without making them lose "that portion of indefiniteness, that opacity and that mystery, which one's actions always have for the one who sees them." It must be said: this genius, Nathalie Sarraute has it. There are few living authors whom I admire as much. Every line of hers is precious. This novelist always comes back to the same theme; what she says corresponds to what our experience has taught us, but as nobody has expressed it before her. I never tire of watching her clear away and cultivate the psychological domain which she has appropriated and where she reigns.

If we consult our dictionary, we see that "tropism" signifies: "Development or progression of an organism in a given direction, under the influence of an exterior stimulus (light, heat, nutritive activity, etc.)." This defines the purpose of Nathalie Sarraute from the time of *Tropismes*— and her originality, anonymous men and women (you, he, she, I) being the organisms subject to these attractions. However, humor is there, muted but alive, discreet but lucid, which changes the known quantities in the problem. The great human problem. Commonplaces: commonplace of all men, humble base of great departures.

Like those authors previously analyzed in this work, Nathalie Sarraute's diagnosis in *L'Ere du Soupçon* blends the personal observations and convictions of all who have reflected about the modern novel, which already exists in embryo but is taking more and more definite shape. Whoever has tried to write a novel himself, or more exactly a novel-essay in this spirit, will find comfort in seeing ideas supported or condemned which, without having read writers' manuals, he, himself, has instinctively sought or shunned. Robbe-Grillet and Cioran have already given him some of those joys that Nathalie Sarraute once more procures for him. All this is in the air. Without having passed the word along, without having peeked over one another's shoulder, we produce compositions in which, despite the lack of satisfactory solutions, we are posing the same problem in similar terms. Again, it is only a matter of approximations of unequal value but of parallel orientation.

Nathalie Sarraute starts with a Stendhal phrase: "The genius of suspicion has come into the world." For her it will be the literary world only. The reader becomes suspicious of what the author tells him as soon as it no longer has to do with direct confidences or he is offered information that is the least bit transposed. As for the novelist, he does not believe to any greater extent in heroes who, little by little, have lost all the attributes, rights, and duties of characters in a novel: not only their civil status (thus in the *Planétarium,* where there is no hero, we pass from one to another without any indication, as from one little derisive and pathetic star to another) but also their physical peculiarities, but also that mark of their irreplaceable personality: character. All the pages written by Mme. Sarraute on this theme are excellent, even though they teach us nothing that we have not already read many times in the books of our colleagues and in ourselves: disappearance of types in the manner of Balzac in favor of some not too concrete props, "hosts of emotional states which, although sometimes still unexplored, we also find in ourselves"; preference given to the true small fact, often of autobiographical origin, exposed without worrying about ridicule; frequent choice of telling the story in the first person; more and more extensive abstraction of secondary characters who became "excrescences, modalities, experiences or dreams of the *I* with whom the author identifies himself," etc. Nathalie Sarraute borrows an illuminating comparison from the plastic domain:

In the same way, modern painting—and one could say that all pictures, since Impressionism, have been painted in the first person —plucks the object from the universe of the spectator and deforms it in order to segregate the pictorial element.

Thus the author of *L'Ere du Soupçon* may with reason salute the birth of a new realism. For certain authors, this realism will end in the precise description of the imprecise, description of a universe where the most solid objects and the most assured thoughts themselves unravel into evanescent and tenuous puffs of smoke. In every way the proposition is Nathalie Sarraute's when she writes that it is up to the author "whatever his desire may be, to amuse his contemporaries or to reform them, to instruct them or to struggle for their emancipation—to seize, forcing himself to cheat as little as possible, to prune and simplify nothing in order to overcome contradictions and complexities, to scrutinize with all the sincerity of which he is capable, as far as the acuteness of his sight permits, what appears to him to be reality."

These novel-essays being what they are (works of writers still groping) and appearing as they appear (read by readers who strive to find old trails once more instead of discovering pathways that are scarcely traced yet indicated), one could advance the idea, according to Cioran, that what authors think of their own endeavors is as important as what they have succeeded in creating. If that is the case, plans are as valuable as constructions. It would be preferable not to look too closely behind the scaffolding. The discreet confidences of a writer about his own novels would probably be as instructive as, and more interesting than, the novels themselves. It is the author, even if he has partially failed, who can teach us best what he wanted to do.

The author of *Portrait d'un inconnu* and *Martereau* was not only concerned with Stendhal and his famous prophecy: ("I shall be understood in 1880"), when she wrote that, in order to succeed in capturing reality, the realistic novelist, in the new and complete sense of the word,

strains relentlessly to discard from what he observes the dross of preconceived ideas and ready-made images which envelop him, all that surface reality that everybody perceives without effort and uses for want of anything better, and now and again he happens to reach something that is still unknown and that it seems to him he is the first to see. He often notices, when he tries to bring to light his bit of reality, that the methods of his predecessors, created for their own purposes, can no longer serve him. So he rejects them without hesitation and strives to find new ones, destined for his own use. Little does it matter to him if at first they disconcert or irritate the reader.

This explains the acceptance by the best authors of the idea of intellectual solitude. Others do not have this courage and, more or less quickly, make concessions. Their characters are not differentiated (it is almost done on purpose); the plan of their work seems disorganized (its relative novelty hides its rigorous design); we are not dealing with a novel (at any rate not in the traditional sense); we pick up from the author contradictory judgments about the same character (elementary and yet still too subtle!). . . . Then the apprentice novelist reintroduces as much as he can (and it is far too much): the marquise, her umbrella and her dog; then he underlines what he had hoped would be guessed at: but by accentuating the features of his book, he deforms it. On the essential, however, he does not give ground. The essential, for Nathalie Sarraute, is what the dialogues at the same time dissemble and confess. (Why not? To each his method. One convention is as good as another.) Whence the importance that she grants to the English novelist Ivy Compton-Burnett, whose books have something absolutely new in that they are a long series of dialogues. Conversation which, according to Mme. Sarraute, is original in this sense, namely, that the subconscious conversation (hidden in reality most of the time) crops up continually, trying to deploy and express itself on the outside.

This notion of subconscious conversation is perhaps not so new as it appears. In Ivy Compton-Burnett herself, where, in *the fierce game* played between the conversation and the sub-conversation, the latter wins most often, it happens "that the ordinary conversation appears to triumph, driving the sub-conversation all the way back. Then, sometimes, at the moment when the reader believes that he can at last relax, the author suddenly emerges from her mutism and intervenes to warn him briefly and without explanation that everything that has just been said is false." Little does it matter of what these new techniques are made. Only the result counts. Nathalie Sarraute defends Ivy Compton-Burnett in order to bolster her own cause. A good cause. Our cause.

CONCLUSION

I HAVE CHOSEN MY AUTHORS ACCORDING TO THE INCLINATION of the moment, because I could not hope to exhaust the subject. In place of Kafka, Artaud, Miller, Beckett, Camus, Michaux, Cioran, Robbe-Grillet, Nathalie Sarraute, I could just as well have discussed Joyce, Roger Gilbert-Lecomte, Faulkner, Blanchot, Sartre, Char, Ponge, Virginia Woolf. No doubt my report would not have differed greatly.

Everything has, with few exceptions, gone forward as though, under various guises, we were dealing with one and the same author, using the same passwords.

Beckett and Camus speak, like Kafka, of *guilt*, and, like Kafka, Bataille and Cioran of *torture*, Michaux of *metamorphoses*. Michaux reached the point of seeing, like Beckett, irrefutable reality in *paralysis*. His notion of *stranger* seems close to that of Albert Camus or Georges Simenon, who again brings us back to Kafka.

If they are not madmen like Artaud or, in a certain sense, like Kafka, most of our authors mimic madness, following the examples of Beckett or Bataille, or seek its substitutes through drugs.

Michaux, like Artaud, wants to free himself from *seizures and exorcisms*. Michaux, in the same way as Kafka and Artaud, refers to his *marrow*. Michaux, in the manner of Joyce, invents words, and, like Joyce, Leiris places his bet on the revelatory value of the *pun*, which gives me the opportunity to mention the kafkastrophic orientation of our writers. Bataille, like Beckett, ends by wanting to destroy what he writes by tying the negation to the affirmation.

Thus a great number of the authors studied here hope to obtain from incoherence the perfection that coherence refuses them. The same shadows envelop them. Meanwhile, painting has reached the point of purifying incandescence where letters are consumed. As Mallarmé kills literature in producing it, Monet denies the art of painting through the power of his art. This evolution is being carried on still farther today, so that what corresponds to *aliterature* should be called *apainting*, and, in another domain, *amusic*.

Whatever conflict there is among the diverse forms of aliterature, we have ascertained broadly that, in contrast with those who unleash language (Artaud, Beckett) are those who tie it down (Camus, Caillois), while certain critics and novelists attempt reconstruction, renouncing the empty shadows and worn-out lights of former times (Robbe-Grillet, Nathalie Sarraute).

Since extreme perfection is unattainable, even the most self-critical writers may be suspected of falling short of their mark. We have already said, in connection with Paul Valéry (whose *desire for precision* did not save him from Julien Benda's criticism) that one is always someone's man of letters. Nathalie Sarraute, in a violent article in *Temps*

Modernes, went even farther in her condemnation of Valéry, to the point of having "to keep from laughing" at "these laborious variations worthy of the *Précieuses Ridicules"*:

And it is thus that a poetical work like *La Jeune Parque* and *Charmes,* swollen with eloquence, rhetoric, false classicism, sprinkled with pretentious affectations, pastiches, platitudes and errors of taste . . . for twenty years, occasioned so few reservations and caused all this swooning.

Paul Valéry, whom we have recognized as one of the forerunners of modern aliterature, is thus struck by the most modern of *alittérateurs,* Nathalie Sarraute, from the list of authors who count. The weak point of aliterary critics and their masters is in the scorn and ignorance that they heap on schools and individuals of an inspiration different from theirs. It suffices to put the new poetical, fictional, and critical theories in their place in literary history (which is also that of aliterature) to re-establish a perspective.

A day will come when the novels of some avant-garde writer will appear as old-fashioned as those scorned by him today. They will remain no less good (if they are good). Creative artists have always been preoccupied with technical questions. But form is distinct from content only in unsuccessful works. All that is needed to renew literature is a new man of letters.

Never pure, the best in aliterature blends with the best in literature. Abandoning our working hypothesis, we can now study *contemporary literature* with an easy conscience, without rejecting or sacrificing any good author, admiring wholeheartedly Roger Martin du Gard and Nathalie Sarraute, Nathalie Sarraute and Paul Valéry.